Praise for *Who Ordered this Truckload of Dung?*

"One of the Best Spiritual Books of 2005. Entertaining and spiritually edifying. Brimming with humor, humanity, and good will." —*Spirituality and Health*

"More than statistics and theories, we really trust anecdotes and narratives. Our brains and beings are wired to learn deeply and easily via stories, and this splendid collection of 108 Buddhist-based tales proves the point. Brahm weaves a rich tapestry of understanding using short threads of stories only a couple of pages long." —*Publishers Weekly*

"A book destined to become dog-eared and cherished and read aloud to friends and family. It will fall apart from your attention, I promise you! It's crammed with pithy, modern 'Buddhist Tales of Happiness,' which cleverly relate the wisdom of Buddha's teachings in a poignant, funny, and profound way." —*Mandala Magazine*

Praise for *Mindfulness, Bliss, and Beyond*

"*Mindfulness, Bliss, and Beyond* demonstrates that Ajahn Brahm is that rare meditator who has actually had—and can describe—the profound meditation experiences outlined in the early Buddhist teachings. The good humor is still present, but this outing is more serious, taking us systematically through the classic stages of meditation training from the most mundane (meditation for happiness) to the most exalted (meditation for enlightenment). Along the way, he gives a thorough description of the jhana states, a place that many Western Buddhist teachers have feared to tread. Ajahn Brahm then brings the whole thing back to the kitchen-sink level with some practical suggestions for everyday life." —*Shambhala Sun*

"Buddhist writers are not often lighthearted or zesty, but the British-born Ajahn Brahm is a delightful exception... Meditation is difficult to teach on the page, but Brahm projects both energetic conviction and calm equanimity. The promise of bliss he describes in this excellent manual is elusive but remains a compelling goal." —*Publishers Weekly*

"Riveting, rollicking, and uncompromisingly real." —Glenn Wallis, translator of *The Dhammapada: Verses on the Way*

THE ART

of

DISAPPEARING

The Buddha's Path to Lasting Joy

Ajahn Brahm

Wisdom Publications • Boston

Wisdom Publications, Inc.
199 Elm Street
Somerville MA 02144 USA
www.wisdompubs.org

Library of Congress Cataloging-in-Publication Data
Ajahn Brahm, 1951–
  The art of disappearing : the Buddha's path to lasting joy / Ajahn Brahm.
    p. cm.
  ISBN 0-86171-668-X (pbk. : alk. paper)
  1. Religious life—Buddhism. I. Title.
  BQ5405.A525 2011
  294.3'444—dc23
                        2011022678
ISBN: 9780861716685
eBook ISBN: 9780861718610

15 14 13 12
5 4 3 2

Cover design by Phil Pascuzzo. Interior design by Gopa&Ted2, Inc.; typset by LC. Set in Diacritical Garamond Pro 11.25/15. Back-cover author photo courtesy of Pagoda Phat Hue, www.phathue.de.

Wisdom Publications' books are printed on acid-free paper and meet the guidelines for permanence and durability of the Committee for Production Guidelines for Book Longevity of the Council on Library Resources.

This book was produced with environmental mindfulness. We have elected to print this title on 30% PCW recycled paper. As a result, we have saved the following resources: 8 trees, 4 million BTUs of energy, 676 lbs. of greenhouse gases, 3,670 gallons of water, and 246 lbs. of solid waste. For more information, please visit our website, www.wisdompubs.org. This paper is also FSC certified. For more information, please visit www.fscus.org. Environmental impact estimates were made using the Environmental Paper Network Paper Calculator. For more information visit www.papercalculator.org.

Contents

◆ ◆ ◆ ─────────────────

Preface

◆ ◆ ◆ ───

D O NOT READ this book if you want to be a somebody. It will
make you a nobody, a no-self.

I did not write this book. They are transcribed talks, edited with all the
bad jokes removed. I did not say my bad jokes anyway. The five *khandhas*, which presumptuously claim to be me, said them. I have the perfect
alibi—my self was absent from the scene of the crime!

This book does not tell you what you must do to get enlightened. It is not
an instruction manual like *Mindfulness, Bliss, and Beyond*, which was also
written by those pesky five *khandhas* pretending to be Ajahn Brahm. Doing
things like following instructions just makes you more of a person. Instead,
this book describes how disappearing happens in spite of you. Moreover, it
is not just the "outside" that vanishes. The entire "inside," all that you take
to be you, that also disappears. And that is so much fun it is sheer bliss.

The true purpose of practicing Buddhism is to let go of everything,
not to get more things like attainments to show off to your friends. When
we let go of something, really let go, then it disappears. We lose it. All
successful meditators are losers. They lose their attachments. Enlightened
ones lose everything. They truly are the *Biggest Loser*. At the very least, if
you read this book and understand some of it, you may discover the meaning of freedom and, as a consequence, lose all of the hair on your head!

I acknowledge the kind assistance of other nobodies, in particular Ron
Storey for transcribing the talks, Ajahn Brahmali for editing the work,
and all the empty beings at Wisdom Publications for publishing the book.

May you all Get Lost,

Not really Ajahn Brahm, Perth, July 2011

The Big Picture 1

WHEREVER YOU LIVE—in a monastery, in a city, or on a quiet tree-lined street—you will always experience problems and difficulties from time to time. This is just the nature of life. So when you have problems with your health you shouldn't say, "Doctor, there is something wrong with me—I'm sick"; rather you should say, "There is something right with me—I'm sick today." It's the nature of the human body to be sick now and again. It's also the nature of the septic system to need pumping out when you don't expect it, and it's the nature of the water heater to sometimes break down. It's the nature of life to be this way. Even though we struggle as human beings to try to make life go smoothly for ourselves and others, nevertheless it's impossible to ensure that happens.

Whenever you experience any pain or difficulty, always remember one of the deep meanings of the word *suffering*: asking the world for something it can never give you. We expect and ask impossible things from the world. We ask for the perfect home and job and that all the things we work hard to build and arrange run perfectly at the right time and place. Of course, that is asking for something that can never be given. We ask for profound meditation and enlightenment, right here and now. But that's not the way this universe works. If you ask for something that the world can't supply, you should understand that you're asking for suffering.

So whether you work or meditate, please accept that things will go wrong from time to time. Your job is not to ask for things the world can't give you. Your job is to observe. Your job is not to try to prod and push this world to make it just the way you would like it to be. Your job is to understand, accept, and let it go. The more you fight your body, your mind, your family, and the world, the more collateral damage you'll cause and the more pain you'll experience.

Sometimes, when we understand and stand back from our daily lives, we see the big picture. We see there's nothing wrong with the monastery, nothing wrong with us, nothing wrong with life. We understand that it's just the nature of the world to go "wrong"—that's what the Buddha meant by the first noble truth of suffering. You work, struggle, and strive so hard to make your life just right—to make your home, your body, and your mind just right—and it all goes wrong anyway.

Understanding Suffering Is the Motivation for Practice

The contemplation of suffering, or *dukkha*, is an important part of true Buddhist practice. We don't try to control suffering; rather, we try to understand it by investigating its causes. It's an important point in our practice, because when most human beings experience suffering, they make the mistake of either running away from it or trying to change it. They blame the machinery for failing, but of course that's just the nature of machinery. Things go wrong and we suffer. So we should change our attitude and stop fighting. When we stop fighting the world and start to understand the suffering, we get another response. It's the response called *nibbidā*.

The response called *nibbidā* comes from understanding the nature of the body, the mind, and the world. You understand the nature of Buddhism, of setting up a monastery or a household, and of living together in a group. You know it's going to be unsatisfactory and that there are going to be problems. You are wise enough to stop running away from those problems or trying to change them. You understand that problems are inherent in the fabric of *saṃsāra*. This was one of the great insights of the Buddha that prompted him to give his first teaching, the *Dhamma-cakkappavattana Sutta* (SN 56:11).

When you realize that suffering is inherent in the fabric of *saṃsāra*, it changes your reaction. It's like having a rotten apple and trying to cut out the rotten parts so you can eat the rest. When you have wisdom, you see that the whole of the apple is rotten and that the only possible response is *nibbidā*—the rejection of the whole apple, revulsion toward it, turning away from it, and just throwing it away. You see that you don't need that apple; you can let it go. It's important to understand the suffering in this world, and it's important to see how absolute that suffering and unsatisfactoriness is. It will never be under your control or within your power to sort it out and get it right.

When we contemplate and understand this, it gives us the motivation and incentive for practicing the path. According to the *suttas*, when the Buddha saw people getting old, getting sick, and dying, that was enough to prompt him to seek a solution to suffering (MN 26.13). He realized that it was also his own nature to get old, get sick, and die, that he had not gone beyond these things. That gave him the motivation to set out in search of an end to these problems.

Each of these three problems is your inheritance too. This is what awaits you in the future. This is something that's certain: you will get old, get sick, and die. There's nothing you can do about that. These are the facts of your existence, your human body, and also all other things. Everything will get old, disintegrate, and die—everything goes wrong and breaks down. The Buddha-to-be was wise enough to know that even with all his spiritual qualities and accumulated merit, he could not avoid that suffering. A different response was needed: to fully understand it.

Disengagement

In the *Dhammacakkappavattana Sutta* it is said that the first noble truth of suffering should be thoroughly understood (SN 56:11). In other words, you don't try to overcome suffering, you don't try to change it, you don't try to make it all better or escape from it; you understand it. Difficult times are wonderful opportunities to sit down and face suffering, to understand it fully and not take the easy option of always running away.

It's the nature of most human beings that whenever suffering or problems arise, they have their escape routes: getting lost in fantasies, watching movies, surfing the internet, reading, chatting, having cups of tea or coffee, or just going for walks. What are we really walking away from? What are we going into those fantasies for? It's our habitual response to the problem of things not being good enough, not being satisfactory. If you really want to get somewhere in life, monastic or otherwise, to become wise and free, the Buddha said you should understand suffering.

When you start to investigate you realize that we all experience suffering. In the *Therīgāthā* there's the famous story of Kisāgotamī (Thī. 213–23). The Buddha's strategy for moving Kisāgotamī away from the grief and suffering caused by the death of her son was to make it quite plain to her that other people die as well: the death of her son was not a solitary event in this universe but was connected to every other death. The Buddha wanted Kisāgotamī to understand the suffering called death. Death is natural; it is part of the fabric of things. It's everywhere; you can't escape it. So instead of trying to solve the problem by bringing her son back to life, the Buddha taught Kisāgotamī to understand the universality of the problem.

When we understand, we don't just accept things, because that's not good enough either. To think, "Just let it be, this is the way things are, so what!" is not the right response. When we really understand the problem of suffering, what we're in for, what life is truly like, there's only one natural response. It's neither trying to escape nor accepting whatever comes; it's *nibbidā*.

Nibbidā means disengaging. We turn away from this thing we call life. Trying to change things just gets you more involved in life, and accepting things also keeps you involved. Disengaging is the right response. Disengaging means you leave these things alone and you're not concerned or worried about them. You just sit there and you don't involve yourself in what you're experiencing. By not involving yourself in what you're experiencing, you stand back from life. It's almost like rejecting it, the sort of rejection that makes things disappear.

You read in the *suttas* that the Buddha, out of compassion, knew how to dismiss people (MN 122.6). Sometimes people will engage in conversation because they have nothing better to do. I don't like sitting around and answering questions hour after hour, particularly during a retreat. In any case, you don't get answers about real *Dhamma* by asking questions. You get those answers by sitting still and stopping your thinking, not by encouraging it further. So when someone asks me a question, I try to make the answer as brief as possible. In this way I try to help people disengage from chitchat.

You should disengage from the things of the world in the very same way. Why be involved in all these things? Look at them and realize they just cause you suffering; they just make you tired and upset. Through *nibbidā* all these sensory objects fade in importance.

"Not My Business"

When you contemplate life you come to realize that it's completely out of control. And whatever is out of control is none of your business. That's a wonderful little saying that I've used in my meditation and that I encourage other people to use as well. Whatever you are experiencing, in the monastery or elsewhere, say to it, "Not my business." Whatever happens to the water supply, to people coming and going, to the food that is offered, to the weather, say to it, "It's not my business." It's not your business to worry about what anyone else does or says to you; it's their business, their *kamma*, nothing to do with you.

If you're sensitive to other people's words and allow them to hurt or bully you, you should remember the Buddha's advice to his son Rahula—to be like the earth (MN 62.13). People urinate and defecate on the earth; they vomit on it and burn it. All sorts of rubbish gets tossed on the earth, but the earth never complains; it just accepts everything. People also do some beautiful things on the earth. They plant gardens or, even better, they build monasteries. But the earth doesn't react no matter what happens to it.

So be like the earth. Whatever people say or do, be immovable. If they praise you or blame you, it's their business. There's no need to be affected by another person's speech, whether good or bad. When you have the attitude of "None of my business," it will never upset you.

It's the same with the aches and pains in the body and with sickness. When you meditate, remind yourself they're none of your business; they're the body's business—let the body look after them. Thinking like that is actually a powerful way of keeping the body healthy. It's a strange thing that sometimes the more you worry about this body, the worse it gets. If you disengage from the body, sit still, and just allow the body to disappear, it tends to heal itself. It seems oftentimes when you try to control and organize things they only get worse, and it's the same with your body. Sometimes, when you let it go and just relax, the body becomes so at ease that it heals itself. So just let go and forget about it.

I've known a lot of monks whose health problems disappeared through the power of their meditation. The first time I saw that was with Ajahn Tate. When I first went to Thailand in 1974, he was in the hospital with incurable cancer. They gave him the best possible treatment, but nothing would work, so they sent him back to his monastery to die. He died twenty-five years later. That's one example of what happens when monks "go back to their monastery to die." They go back and then live a long time. So you disengage from things—*nibbidā* arises—and the mind turns away. It's had enough, it doesn't even want to look at them anymore, and you find that they fade away.

This is the process you read about in the *suttas*, *nibbidā* leading to *virāga*, the fading away of things. When you regard something as none of your business, it fades away from your world. Consciousness doesn't engage with it anymore; it doesn't see, hear, feel, or know it. The way this works is as follows. Whatever you engage with is what takes hold in the mind—it's where consciousness finds a footing and grows. You are building mental edifices. It's very clear to me as a meditator that we create our own world. But when you disengage, you have no business there, and because you're not interested in it, the whole thing just disappears from your consciousness. When you have *nibbidā* you're really "un-creating" your world.

Solving the Problem

How many times have you tried to solve "the problem"? You'll be trying to solve it not just until you die but for many more lifetimes. Instead, understand that this world is just the play of the senses. It's the five *khandhas* doing their thing; it has nothing to do with you. It's just people being people, the world being the world.

Sometimes at our monastery you can see large flocks of cockatoos. They are very noisy. Some people say they don't like the sound of cockatoos, but whether you like them or not, they still make the same noise, so why not disengage?

As a meditator I used to ask myself, "Why does noise disturb me?" Whether it's the sound of a bird outside or somebody coughing or slamming the door in the main hall, why do I hear that? Why can't I do the same as I do with my eyes, find some "lids" and shut my ears? Through contemplating sound and understanding how it works, it became quite clear that the only reason I heard it was because I went out to listen to it. There was an active engagement with the world of sound. That's why it was disturbing. Ajahn Chah used to say that it's not the sound that disturbs you; it's you who disturbs the sound. That was a very profound saying, and it meant a lot to me. I used that to understand the nature of sound and why it's so disturbing.

When someone calls you a pig, an idiot, or whatever, you don't need to listen to it. We hear it because we're interested in it; we engage with and are attached to the world of sound. But when we realize that sounds just come according to their nature, we get *nibbidā*. There are nice sounds, crazy sounds, and the sounds of the birds. Some birds sound sweet and some birds, like crows, sound terrible. But it's not the fault of the crows; it's just their nature. It's the same in the monastery: some *anagārikas* are like crows and some are like nightingales; some monks speak beautifully, some speak terribly. It's their nature, that's all. It has nothing to do with us, and therefore we should disengage.

When we disengage from these things through *nibbidā*, they fade away. Suffering fades away when the cause of the suffering fades away. The sense world starts to disappear when we're not so concerned with changing it.

When we disengage from it with *nibbidā*, we're repelled by it and reject it. This is because *nibbidā* comes from seeing the world as it actually is. With it, we move in a different direction from the rest of the world.

The Messengers of Truth

Another way to look at this disengagement from the world is to regard it as a movement into the mind, our silent center. Sometimes you can see how the world of your home, the world of your friends, or even of Buddhism, can pull you out of your center. You can feel the pull. You've been pulled out like that your entire life, and what has it ever done for you? When people leave the monastery, it's usually because of the opposite sex. Is that going to make them happy? Many years ago the title of the main feature of *Punch* magazine was "Advice for those about to be married." The two center pages were blank except for the four letters "DON'T." They had understood the suffering of marriage. Don't think that you're different, that you can escape the suffering because you're special or wiser than others. It's the arrogance of the ego to think that you're better, that you can avoid the difficulties and problems that everyone else faces in life.

When I was young I too used to have fantasies. I learned to stop them from grabbing hold of me by following them to their logical conclusion. I would think, "Then what? Then what?" and I wouldn't stop until I had the full picture. With fantasies such as falling in love, getting married, and riding off into the sunset, the "then what" took all the fun out of it, because the "then what" was just empty. There was no color, brightness, joy, or happiness anymore, because the "then what" would be whatever everyone else experiences. When the fun part dissipates and fades away, you're back where you started. Moreover, you haven't understood anything about life. You're just trying to get by, to get a few moments of pleasure and happiness. In the end you're just hurtling toward old age and separation from those you love. What's the point? But if you follow the path of *nibbidā*, you're wise. You've already experienced enough suffering, which means you have enough data to work with. Reflect on that suffering when you have difficulties and build up the *nibbidā*.

During a retreat, you will have times when you get bored. If you've got aching legs or you're just sitting there not knowing what to do—you don't want to meditate, walk, or read, and you're bored out of your skull—investigate boredom. If you investigate suffering, there's no moment of a retreat that you can't make use of, that you can't exploit for your own personal growth and training. The training of the mind is not in controlling things but in understanding them. Look upon the difficulties and disappointments as *devadūtas*, the messengers of truth that come to teach you *Dhamma*. Ajahn Chah always called these things the Kruba Ajahns—the senior teachers. Kruba Ajahns don't live in Thailand in some great monastery. That's a fantasy Kruba Ajahn. The true Kruba Ajahn will be in your hut when you wake up in the morning and you're so tired that you don't want to get out of bed. Those Kruba Ajahns will be there when you're sitting for long periods of time and getting absolutely nowhere. The real Kruba Ajahn will be there when you're on retreat wondering how many days are left. When somebody doesn't put the right food in your bowl, or you're just about to get into deep meditation and a crow makes a loud noise, or whatever else it is that really disappoints and frustrates you—that's an Ajahn. It's to be contemplated, listened to, penetrated, and understood.

Moving toward Emptiness

When you understand the suffering in the world, you see the world as a load of rubbish. Because it's rubbish you disengage. When you disengage, it fades away; that is, *virāga* happens. This is nature. You don't have to make it fade away. It's not done by choice or by will or by thinking, "Oh, I want to get rid of these people, these crows, these ants on the path, this cold that I feel." You don't want to get rid of anything. It's just not your business anymore. When you truly know that it's none of your business, the whole thing just fades and disappears. This is the deeper meaning of simplifying and renouncing one's possessions. You don't just renounce physical things but also your "mental possessions"—the old habits and grudges, the old ways of looking at things that you hang on to and cherish. You abandon all the things that wear you down, that confine and limit you.

Most people are prisoners of their past. They identify with the past, regarding it as their self, their *attā*. Since they take themselves to be the past, it becomes their business, and they attach to it and suffer accordingly. But they don't have to; they can let go of the past. The door of that prison cell is always open, and you can walk through it at any time. Don't think that you have to work through the "issues" of the past—that's just guilt. You can completely let go of all that, abandon it, and allow it to vanish if you have the guts to do so.

So using *dukkha-saññā*, the perception of suffering, ask yourself what the point is of holding on to your past. See it for what it is; understand that it's suffering, disengage, and allow it to fade away. You don't even think of your past anymore. When you understand that these things are suffering, renunciation happens as a direct result, and the deeper the understanding, the more they fade. Eventually they're just not part of your repertoire anymore. You look at the world outside and it fades away; you sit in your hut and the whole world disappears. You understand that this is what meditation is all about. Meditation is the art of letting things disappear and fade, letting them vanish. It's a movement toward emptiness.

One of the most important things that must fade for meditation to take off is thinking. Firstly you must understand thinking. You must objectify it and see it for what it truly is. Where does thinking get you? You will see that thinking is none of your business. When you understand thinking properly, you don't try to control it through an act of will but you have *nibbidā* toward it. To use a simile from the *suttas* (e.g., MN 20.4), regard thinking as the carcass of a dead dog around the neck of your beautiful mind. Once you look at it in that way, you wonder why you are doing this to yourself. The automatic reaction is to throw it out, just as you would the carcass of a dead dog—rotten, dirty, smelly, and foul. This is what happens when you understand these things. You know they're none of your business. You reject them, or rather rejection happens. You move in another direction—into the mind rather than out into the world.

America - Imagine the
world w/o her.

Dinesh D'Souza

2016: Obama's America

The Automatic Reaction

Nibbidā stops the *āsavas*, the outflowings of the mind. You know what it's like: you're sitting there in meditation doing nothing, and suddenly thinking starts flowing out—about what you're going to do after the retreat, about your duties, or about the answer to some problem you're trying to solve. The mind flows out from its center, and it's this flowing out that's called an *āsava*. Why does it flow out? It flows out because it's interested in the world. It hasn't seen the suffering of the world, it hasn't understood it. When you haven't understood the world outside, you think it's your business—you think it's fun, that you're going to get something from your studies or from arranging all these things of the world. But when you disengage, all that fades away, and the *āsavas*—the outflowings—stop. The sense that the world is important disappears, because you understand it's none of your business. When the world outside goes, past and future and thinking also disappear, and then your meditation takes off.

When you disengage from the outside, meditation just happens. It's important to realize that you don't make it happen. I don't like it when people teach others to use willpower to watch the breath. It's better to use wisdom power. Through wisdom you see that the world is suffering, and then you disengage, you get *nibbidā*. You can't do anything else; it's an automatic reaction. So understanding suffering and disengaging are the base that you always come back to. And the more you disengage the easier it is to meditate. When I say easier, it's just that meditation happens, that's all.

As you disengage from the world you go inside, and you're in the present moment. You may be watching the breath, but as you come to understand it, you disengage even from the breath. You don't try to control the breath or make it different. The breath comes in and goes out all by itself, and you realize the breath is none of your business. You get *nibbidā* toward it, too, and it fades away. According to the Buddha, watching the breath is part of body contemplation (MN 118.24). So when you see that the breath has nothing to do with you and you disengage from it, it's really the remnants of the physical body and the five senses that fade and disappear. That's when you start to get into the deep stuff. Because the body and its five senses are gone at last, your meditation is deep, and you're having a great time.

When you disengage from suffering, not trying to control the world, not trying to stay there, just letting things be, you get what you really wanted in the first place: peace and happiness. Why do people struggle with this world in their pursuit of happiness? Or do you think just going along with it is going to make you happy? That just makes you bored and dull, sometimes even depressed. Only the way of *nibbidā* leads to true happiness of the mind. You're still and peaceful because so much has disappeared.

Only now can you fully appreciate that it was all just suffering in the first place. The five senses are suffering, this world is suffering. Speech and thinking are suffering. Monasteries are suffering, rain is suffering, study is suffering, and whatever you're doing is suffering. Food is suffering. Everything is suffering. When you disengage and go inside to the place where Māra can't reach, there's a beautiful freedom from suffering. This is the way into the deep meditation states called *jhāna*: you disengage from the world; you don't engage with *jhāna*. When you disengage from thinking, from the world and the body, *jhāna* just happens. It's another automatic reaction, and it occurs when you understand that all of these things are none of your business.

Stillness

I've been trying to keep this body of mine fit and healthy for a long time: I've been washing it, caring for it, and resting it. But when I meditate I say, "None of my business." I just sit there and disengage completely. Even though I am the abbot, I disengage from my monastery and from everything else. When I go inside my cave, I've got nothing to do. I'm not my body, not my past or future. I just sit there and allow everything to fade, vanish, and go.

Disengaging like that, experiencing *nibbidā*, leads to *virāga*. *Virāga* in turn leads to *upasama*—stillness, calm, peace. It's a beautiful thing to

Notes For the
Future Buddhism
Study

Dhammacakkapp-
avattana Sutta
(SN 56:11)

just a note...

Re read
" Not my Business

Re read
The Automatic Reaction

Re read Chapter 3 need to parts on
mindfullness.
Anāpānsati Sutta (Mn 118.17)
    meditator has to establish mindfulness

know the true peace of mind where the whole world outside vanishes and you're absolutely still. The mind is motionless and cannot connect with the body or with past and future. It's motionless in time and motionless in space, and that stillness allows everything to fade away and disappear. Things only exist when there is some movement or agitation, because the senses only know things when they move. For the senses to know anything, they need comparison, they need contrast. When they're still, the unity makes things fade: the whole world outside fades, the monastery fades, sounds fade, memories fade, past and future and thinking fade, and the body disappears.

When the body disappears and you experience stillness deep inside, it's a *jhāna* state. In that *jhāna* state you're disengaged from the world outside—the five senses have vanished. Sometimes this is called being "aloof" from the world of the five senses. In fact it's more than aloofness; it's complete disengagement, the complete ending of that world. Now you understand the meaning of vanishing, of things not being there anymore. Now you know what renunciation truly is. You renounce the world, and it's so much fun, so peaceful. I say renouncing, but really you've done nothing. Disengagement has occurred through understanding the world, because the natural consequence of understanding is *nibbidā*. Things fade away, and you get a beautiful peace, the stillness of the mind.

Once you start to taste the stillness in the mind, it's terribly addictive. It's meant to be. It's a good thing because the addiction of the mind to stillness is what's going to drive you deeper toward *nibbāna*. The Buddha actually said that attachment to deep meditation can lead only to the stages of enlightenment (DN 29). You don't have to be concerned or worried about the addiction to letting go. This is the pleasure, joy, and path of monastics. It's their freedom. It's an addiction that leads to more and more fading away and letting go. *Nibbidā* increases and it pushes you away from the world.

This is what it is to be a true monastic, a *bhikkhu* or *bhikkhunī*. Now you know why we follow this Buddhist path. You know how there can be these amazing people who walk this path, who disengage from the world and allow it to fade away. They spend hour after hour happily by themselves, their "selves" actually disappearing. They go deeper and deeper inward, not because they move themselves inward but because they see that the suffering surrounding them is none of their business. They disengage, and things just fade and fade and fade away.

Understanding Is the Key

To meditate you don't need to fix your mind on the breath, to deliberately let go of the past and the future, or to silence the thinking mind. Just contemplate suffering and understand it right now, through whatever you're experiencing. Through that understanding you'll find that the world disappears. The world in which you used to play will fade in importance; you won't visit that playground anymore. The playground of the senses, of the past and future, of sex and dreams, will fade away. It happens not because you make it happen but because this is the natural reaction of the mind when it sees suffering. As all this fades away, meditation takes its place. You don't become a meditator; meditation just happens. It's a path, a route, and these are signposts on the journey, landmarks on the road to complete emptiness and cessation. It's what happens when you disengage and let go.

The Buddha said suffering is to be fully understood. Whenever you experience any difficulties, problems, disappointments, or any mental or physical pain, please don't reject it; understand it. Don't just leave it alone: contemplate it and understand it so well that it fades, and you realize it's none of your business. When it fades away, your engagement with the world outside will be broken, and you'll start to engage with the inner world. You go in the opposite direction, not out into the world but into the mind. Eventually you also let go of the mind, experiencing complete cessation and *nibbāna*, and then you'll be another *arahant*. What a wonderful thing that would be.

Bringing the Mind into the Present 2

◆ ◆ ◆

WHEN YOU'RE ON A LONG RETREAT you need to be very gentle. You should relax and ease yourself in. Little by little, as you go further into the retreat, you tend to get into a beautiful routine. You experience how wonderful it is to have most of the day to yourself.

However, when you have an ideal situation, when the externals are virtually clear of hindrances and obstacles, you soon find that the biggest hindrances and obstacles are presented by the mind. You may experience boredom, restlessness, sleepiness, or frustration when you have so much time to yourself. Nevertheless, it's important to devote that time to meditation. Without the solitude and the time to face the mind, you'll never realize that those obstacles exist in the first place.

Mindfulness of the Body and Caring Attention

One of the meditation techniques that is good to use—especially if you are busy—is mindfulness of the body. When you get disturbed it's often hard to settle down again. Instead of going straight to present-moment awareness, silence, the breath, *mettā*, or whatever other type of meditation you use, sit down and just become aware of the sensations and feelings in your body. Focusing on the physical feelings is a way of giving ease to those feelings. This is particularly useful if you are tired or sick. And it's not that hard.

To make this sort of practice truly effective, use caring attention. Caring attention is not just being mindful but also looking upon those feelings with gentleness and compassion. You're not just aware of the sensations, but you're kind and gentle with them. Kindness and gentleness, along with mindfulness, make it easier both to engage with the object and to calm and tranquilize it. For example, if you have aches in the knees or some sort of tension in the body, you'll find that using mindfulness, plus a little bit of compassion for yourself, makes it easy to maintain your attention on the body.

I find this sort of practice very useful for things like walking meditation. When I'm doing walking meditation, after a while my body starts to get hot, and sometimes when I sit down it's a bit tired and achy. The physical feelings I experience are very prominent; they're loud and easy to focus on. This gives you an easy object to start your meditation with, which stops the mind from drifting off somewhere else. It also calms the body down when making the transition from the active walking meditation to the inactive sitting meditation. It's a beautiful way of focusing and not losing your mindfulness.

To focus on an ache or a pain with caring attention also helps to settle it down. My own experience has shown me that focusing on painful or sick feelings in the body with caring attention tends to lessen them. They seem to respond not just to the awareness directed toward them but to the kindness with which you view them. Take the chanting that monks do for sick people. If you focus on those people and spread loving kindness or *mettā* toward them, it seems to have a positive effect. Imagine what that type of *mettā* can do for you. Because you're far closer to yourself than to anyone else, spreading this caring attention to parts of your own body can have a huge effect on you physically. And sometimes, especially when you get into deep meditation and your mind is very powerful, you can see that it works. You can "zap" an ache with kindness and it disappears straight-away because your mind is so strong. Just put your attention there with some kindness and it works almost immediately. The mindfulness, together with *mettā* and compassion, has surprising power. During any retreat, if you have any sickness, aches, or pains—and you'll have more and more as you get older—use caring attention. Later on, when you sit and watch your breath, this practice will be of great benefit.

By watching the feelings in the body—whatever feelings are present at that particular time—and caring about them, you are actually practicing what I call "present-moment awareness in silence." When you're watching the sensations in the body, silent awareness of the present moment happens all by itself. There isn't much to say about these sensations, whether they're pleasant or painful. It's because they do not engender conversations, concepts, or language that they're a great meditation object for calming down the thinking mind. By getting in contact with feelings rather than thinking, you create a very useful bridge between the outside world and present-moment awareness in silence, and then to the awareness of the breath.

Using Body Sweeping to Calm Restlessness

I've found that body sweeping is a useful technique for people who are restless. It was one of the meditations I introduced at a recent retreat and the meditators loved it. They were mainly executives, very busy people. They were so restless that giving them something to do proved very beneficial. Slowly noticing the feelings in the body from the toes all the way up to the head really calmed them down. It was an active meditation but it was focused in the moment. There was not much thinking that could go on, and so by the end of the sweeping they were actually quite calm—surprisingly so. Of course, those who knew how to go further carried on from there, and I was pleased that some people got into very nice meditation for the first time.

It's always a great joy as a teacher when students understand what meditation is like for the first time. It is marvelous when someone says, "It was so easy and I got so focused. I couldn't hear anything. I was just really inside myself. It was so nice." The people who get deep meditation are sometimes the ones I least expect it of. It's truly wonderful, and sometimes it all starts with body meditation.

Having seen those results, I want to encourage this sort of practice. When you're meditating, don't just sit there and do nothing or fall asleep. Don't just sit there and say, "present-moment awareness," and then start thinking about all sorts of things. Try to develop the body meditation. It's not about understanding the nature of the body. That's a type of body contemplation that I don't think is very useful until after you get into deep meditation. Instead, just be aware of the feelings in the body. Give yourself another technique in your meditation repertoire to use during a long retreat day.

When you have different ways of meditating, you tend not to get bored, which can happen at the beginning of a retreat especially. If you develop present-moment awareness in silence early on by using techniques like body meditation, after a while the meditation starts to bite, to become naturally inclined toward the present moment, toward silence. The more you incline toward something and the more you train yourself in that practice, the more natural it becomes. This is what we mean by training the mind; that's how it works. It's just like people training in tennis. Their coach hits the ball to the same part of the court, and they do a forehand stroke again and again and again. They repeat the same action innumerable times, and because they keep repeating the same action over and over, it becomes habitual. In the same way, by developing present-moment awareness in silence often, it becomes habitual.

The Importance of Joy

Once you get to the silent awareness of the present moment, meditation becomes joyful. That joy—the happiness, the interest, the fun—is one of the most important meditation experiences. It's what keeps you on the cushion and what keeps you from getting bored or restless, thinking, "Gee, there are another two and a half months left of this retreat; how am I going to survive?" That happens because you are not getting any happiness from your meditation. When the happiness comes, you think, "Wow, another two and a half months of this? Ah, bliss!"

Joy in meditation doesn't come from using willpower or force, or from having lots of aspirations and expectations. Joy comes from stillness. By practicing caring awareness of your body, you're generating the ability to be alert to what you're doing. And because you're caring, you're not so forceful. That's when joy can arise.

By developing this caring, you're also avoiding the negativity and fault-finding that cause so many problems in meditation practice. Sometimes we get so negative that we start thinking, "I can't do this. It's hopeless: the teaching is hopeless; the religion is hopeless; life is hopeless." All that negativity is obviated by caring attention. Because of your caring attention, you get a beautiful, open, and gentle mind. If you find that you're looking at the feelings in the body with negativity, just "massage" or "caress" the negative thoughts with caring attention. When you massage negative thoughts and feelings, you avoid making a huge problem out of them.

The Faculty of Mindfulness

Apart from caring, attention is also important. Attention is the supervisor: you watch what you're doing, and you understand the way the mind is moving. Without mindfulness—if you're just fantasizing, or even falling asleep—you don't know what's going on, so you're just wasting your time. It's much better to have half an hour of focused meditation, when you're really paying attention, than to sit for hours being dull or scattered. By developing awareness using the feelings in the body, that aspect of meditation, that particular skill and strength of mind, is being encouraged. By the time you let go of the feelings in the body, mindfulness has been encouraged and generated; it's sharp. Then when you move on to watch the present moment or the silence, the mindfulness is already there.

Mindfulness watches the breath. You know if the attention starts to move away from the breath, and you can bring it back again. This function of mindfulness I call "the gatekeeper." The gatekeeper watches out for enemies. He allows entry only to that which is supposed to enter. In the simile of the gatekeeper (e.g., AN 7:67), the gatekeeper to the city has been told exactly who is allowed to come in and who the enemies are. Obviously, if the gatekeeper is half asleep, all the instructions in the world won't work. On the other hand, if the gatekeeper is fully aware and he carefully watches the robbers going in and going out, that's no good either.

The gatekeeper has to both be fully aware and also know the instructions. It's the same with mindfulness: it has to be sharp to see what's happening, and it has to follow the instructions of where and how to watch. It's like having this observer overlooking everything you do. If mindfulness finds that there's not enough care or you are drifting off, it can take remedial action. This is called the faculty of mindfulness, the *indriya* of *sati*, and it's important to build that up.

Sometimes during meditation you're tired and fall asleep, particularly if you have eaten too much or you've been very busy. Sometimes your body goes through cycles; you go through high and low stages of energy. Sometimes you are just tired and that's it. If it's not the time to sleep, then just sit there and make peace with your tiredness. You may not be all that mindful, but please don't fight the tiredness. When you just sit there without fighting, you don't waste your energy in negativity. Instead you open the door of your heart, and you are kind to your tiredness, and then it usually doesn't last very long.

Some of the tiredness can be just laziness. However, there's an important difference between laziness and genuine tiredness. With laziness you're not developing mindfulness—you're just allowing yourself, probably out of negativity, to go off into what you think is an escape from real life. But if you have some wisdom, you know it's not a very nice escape— dullness is not a pleasant state. It's much better to develop more mindfulness by doing things like watching the body. When mindfulness is stronger, you feel much better, and you can watch the present moment, the silence, or the breath—in short, you can meditate. Because you can meditate, you get more confidence and happiness. It's important, especially when you first start with meditation, to know that, yes, you *can* meditate, you *can* do it. Once you realize that you can meditate, you get the encouragement and motivation to take it deeper.

The worst and most difficult part of meditation is the first part—that is, before you get to the joyful full awareness of the breath, which I often call the *beautiful breath*. This part of meditation can seem boring or uninteresting. Sometimes it's hard work and you get frustrated. But once you get to the beautiful breath, which is the pivot point of meditation, then you're away. So at the beginning make it your goal to develop to that stage and have the confidence that you can do it. Once you get there the teacher isn't so important anymore. All he needs to do now is give you precise instructions on how to take your meditation deeper. You learn fast because you're interested in the meditation and you want to meditate. You're fascinated by the way meditation works, and it becomes like a hobby that you just can't spend enough time on. You're having fun with it.

Mindfulness is important not just during meditation; it should be developed throughout the day. When you're eating, for example, try to be mindful of what you're doing. There's no need to think or talk. A useful practice is to focus on one spoonful at a time. Instead of having one morsel in your mouth and another on your spoon like most people do, just focus on what you are eating right now. When you go to the toilet don't take a book; just watch what it's like to urinate or excrete. By practicing in this way, establishing mindfulness on the ordinary things of the day, when you sit down to meditate it's much easier to be mindful of the body and eventually the breath. So you build up the practices that allow meditation to happen. Little by little you build up the "muscles" of the mind, like kindness and awareness. Meditation becomes far easier: you just sit there and the mind calms down.

Calming Down the Problems

A calm mind is a beautiful, wonderful thing. When the mind is full of thoughts and wanders around, sooner or later you get into negativity. It's very hard to have a thinking mind that is always positive, because thinking tends to degenerate into negativity and fault-finding. You know what happens when you have a lengthy conversation: you may start off talking about high things, but sooner or later the conversation turns negative. The same thing happens with thinking; so be careful of that.

The quieter you become the more happiness you have. So your whole focus should be on calming things down. Don't forget the compassion, because it too has a calming effect. Kindness and compassion smooth over the problems and soothe the hurt. Kindness creates calm since it carries with it the quality of *samatha*, of calming and pacifying things. It especially calms your body down, which is why giving caring attention to feelings tranquilizes them; aches and pains in the muscles and bones and even restlessness tend to disappear. And when you direct kindness and compassion to your mind in the form of caring attention, it tends to calm and soothe any difficulties, problems, or angst you may have. The caring attention is saying, "Ah, never mind, it'll be alright. You don't have to worry about these things. You'll be okay." So you calm everything down, and in that calmness you are free from the tyranny of thought and the pain of negativity.

Negativity is an awful thing to live with. But you always have the option of turning the mind away from negativity, fault-finding, anger, misery, upset, or depression and directing it toward something that is peaceful, calm, and energetic. When you do this with caring attention and you actually care for the present moment, the present moment is not so bad. When you smile at people they smile back, and when you care for them they usually care back. So if you care for this moment it becomes much nicer.

Our state of mind imbues whatever object we're attending to with the corresponding qualities, and that's what we see in the object. If you've got negativity, anything you look at is awful and negative, and it's hard to stay with this moment because it's not nice. This has nothing to do with the nature of the present moment, only with the way you're attending to it. It's the caring aspect of caring attention that turns the present moment into the pleasant moment, making it easy to watch. You don't need to go off into the past or the future or get restless, because you're having a good time here and now. It's the same with silence. When you care for the silence of the mind—the emptiness, the space between words—it becomes beautiful. And because you care and it's beautiful, you can stay there. Your meditation is building and you're getting somewhere. You feel good; you feel, "Wow, I really am a meditator!"

Getting the Results Changes Everything

Never meditate for results. Even though we all want results, even though we want to see things happen, the very act of wanting will block them. Instead, just practice the path with caring attention, thereby putting the causes in place, and the results will come as a matter of course. These results in turn give you positive reinforcement that meditation works and that you can do it. It feels wonderful, and because there's a feeling of greatness, wonder, beauty, and satisfaction, there's a sense that you're getting somewhere. That also feels good. There's a kind of snowball effect.

It's because of caring attention that you can do present-moment awareness and you can do breath meditation. You can watch the breath going in and out for long periods of time, and you know the causes that make it happen. The cause is not willpower but mindfulness and care, and knowing how the process works. You care for the breath; you have kindness toward it and toward yourself, and you have mindfulness. Then the breath is pleasant and easy to watch.

You see that the quality of the breath is a good reflection of the mind. If you're tense, the breath is tense. If you're angry, the breath is very shallow and fast. If a man sees a girl he likes, sometimes he can hardly breathe. You can see how emotions of lust, ill will, or anger really do affect your breathing. So if you watch the breath with caring attention, it makes meditation much easier. When you're kind to the breath you get a kind breath in return. If you smile at the breath, the breath smiles back and becomes pleasant.

Once you get to the pleasant breath, you're on your way. The breath becomes so nice that you just want to watch it. You may have heard these things many times before, even to the point of boredom, but now you are actually doing it. You get peaceful, and the prospect of a long retreat doesn't fill you with dread anymore—it's like being on holiday. The meditation builds, grows, and blossoms, and you have the most wonderful time of your life. The more you watch the breath go in and out, the more still and peaceful you become. Remember: calming and tranquilizing the mind is the whole point of meditation.

Don't go looking for insights at this stage. Don't get into thinking and trying to understand things. Understand stillness—just that one thing. The great thinkers in this world can think, but they don't necessarily have a deep understanding. There are very few people who can get their minds still and peaceful, so become one of those few. See how much stillness you can create, or rather, allow to occur, in your mind. The truly calm mind is so still that hardly anything happens in it. Don't be afraid of the dullness that initially may be a result of the stillness. The dullness soon disappears, and the stillness becomes vibrant, powerful, and full of energy. The still energy—that's the one to go for. In deep meditation there's absolutely no motion, and you've got more energy than a nuclear reactor.

It's a gradual practice. As the mind does less, it has more energy, and in time the mindfulness becomes incredibly powerful. With the power comes great brightness—a naturally caring and energetic brightness. When you have happiness and the compassion that comes with it, it's easy to go deep into the beautiful breath meditation. You've gone past the pivot point; the "climbing" is over. You don't need to put forth effort; as you let go more and more, the meditation just happens. It's at this stage that the ability to really let go of the doer—the controller, the thinker, the maker—becomes paramount. Try it and see what happens.

Understanding the Buddha

If you go back to the *suttas* and see what the Buddha said, you find that your experience matches how the Buddha described things. Then you become a real Buddhist, not just a superficial or intellectual one. You understand what the Buddha taught and how the Buddha lived, and how he calmed his mind and mental faculties to become still, peaceful, and supremely happy. Such practice is reflected in your health, attitude, and life. You become a happier, more effective human being. And eventually you'll be able to share all the energy, wisdom, compassion, understanding, and experience you get from your practice. Then you become a teacher, or you just teach by the example of who you are. Either way, it's really worthwhile.

Developing Mindfulness 3

+ + +

WHEN WE'RE PRACTICING MEDITATION and living our daily lives, one of the most important qualities to understand and develop is mindfulness. If you don't have mindfulness when you're sitting on your cushion or walking on your meditation path, you're basically out of control. If no one is at the steering wheel, the vehicle just veers all over the place and may crash or go off the road.

Mindfulness is what the Buddha called a controlling faculty. It needs to be developed because without it, there can't be any development of stillness. Many years ago, when I was still an inexperienced meditator, sometimes half an hour would go by without my knowing what I was doing. Because my mindfulness wasn't sharp, I would fall into old habits like drowsiness or boredom. Mindfulness is the most important of the faculties for stopping these old habits from returning.

In addition to awareness, you have to understand what you're supposed to be doing—you need the instructions, the will, and the inclination to do what is required. Having the motivation is important, since if you don't feel like training the mind, it simply won't happen. But when you have the mindfulness, the understanding of the instructions, and the motivation together, chances are you will get somewhere in your meditation.

Understanding Mindfulness

To cultivate and nurture mindfulness, you have to understand what it is. People have many different ideas about mindfulness, but they often forget that mindfulness has many different strengths and qualities. In just one day mindfulness can vary from being dull, like a fog where you can't see clearly, to being sharp and fully alert, like a brightly lit room. If you have experienced deep meditation you know how powerful mindfulness can be. There really is such a thing as a very sharp and penetrating mindfulness, and that's what we need to develop. The way to do this is by training the mind.

In the previous chapter I mentioned mindfulness of the body. Developing mindfulness of the body is a relatively easy first step and, as an additional bonus, it may improve your health. As you start off, the more sensations there are in the body, the easier it is to develop mindfulness. But because of that diversity, mindfulness cannot get very strong. To develop powerful mindfulness you have to be aware of simple and precise objects. You grow mindfulness in the same way that you grow a tree. You start with a little seedling, but eventually you have a huge piece of timber that is very strong and powerful. In the same way, you start with ordinary mindfulness, but then you build it up.

It's important to remember that mindfulness can only really exist in the present moment, and with a silent mind. Moment-by-moment awareness should be your initial goal. Don't name things. When you give something a name you're not really aware of the thing; you're only aware of its label. Unfortunately, people with a Western education have been brainwashed into giving things labels and names. They don't see things as they actually are; they're just mindful of the words that describe them. That means mindfulness doesn't really penetrate.

Establishing Mindfulness

As you make present-moment awareness and silence important goals, you find that mindfulness starts to increase and that you become sharper, more aware, and more able to see deeply into things. You're waking up. But it requires training. There are many tricks you can use. Ask yourself, "Where am I?" "What am I doing?" "What am I up to?" A good example of this technique is the way we used to do walking meditation at Wat Pah Pong in Thailand. Ajahn Chah always used to remind us at the start:

Know that you are at this end of the path. When you reach the other side, know that you are at the far end of the path. Next, establish mindfulness at the beginning and end of one particular section of your walking path. Even if your mindfulness wanders off in the middle of that section, at least you bring your mind back to the present moment at the beginning and the end. The next stage is to be mindful in every part of the walking meditation.

It's very useful to establish this sort of mindfulness because you're training yourself to be mindful while you're active. Then you may be able to be mindful when you're eating or in the kitchen washing up. You're actually present with what you're doing rather than trying to get it over with or thinking about something else. Mindfulness really develops when you put one hundred percent attention into what you're doing now, not thinking about what you're going to do next.

When you train like this—putting everything into the moment— you're developing attentive energy that is focused on the now. If you're writing a letter, focus all your energy on writing that letter. If you're meditating in your hut, focus all your energy on that. By putting your attentive energy into one thing at a time, it doesn't blur into the next activity. When one activity is finished, drop it very quickly; don't allow one thing to blend into another. As soon as you sit down, you're doing sitting meditation. When you're on the toilet, you're just on the toilet. When you're brushing your teeth, you're just brushing your teeth. Whatever you're doing, put all your attention into that activity. It's not a waste of time or a preliminary practice.

When you put your energy into focusing on this moment, you're developing mindfulness. By watching out for inner speech and trying to stop it early on, by developing moments of silence and extending those moments of silence, you're improving your ability to just be here— attentive, knowing, and aware. You're abiding in the moment—not going anywhere, not rushing off into the future. Because the mind is silent, you're totally passive and receptive to whatever is happening.

Being passive and receptive is not only a good description of mindfulness, but also a prescription for increasing that mindfulness. In fact, one of the basic principles of mindfulness is that its intensity, its energy, is built on stillness. The more still you are, the more mindfulness increases, and the sharper it becomes. By allowing the thinking process to end and not giving things a name, most of the movement of the mind stops. This creates the stillness that gives rise to energetic mindfulness. That's why these states, where there is little inner conversation, feel so powerful.

If your mindfulness is sharp, you can catch thoughts as soon as they arise, when they're still easy to stop. But once you get into a fantasy, conversation, or plan, the thinking process gains momentum and becomes much harder to stop. It's just like a train. Although a train is heavy, if it has just started to move out from the station it's easy to stop, because it's still moving slowly. But once that train is hurtling along at one hundred kilometers an hour, it takes a long time to stop, simply because the momentum is so great. In the same way, don't allow the thinking mind to build up momentum; stop it before it starts traveling too fast. If you stop the thinking at this early stage, your mindfulness will not dissipate, but will actually increase.

Getting mindfulness started is the hard part, because you don't really know what you're doing and you can't see clearly. Once you've got mindfulness going, you're more aware and alert, and because you see what's happening more clearly, it's easier to stop the thinking process and remain in the present moment. It's just like being in a very dark room: you can't even see well enough to put the light on. However, once you have a little bit of light, you can see the switch to increase it. Mindfulness and awareness are the light of the mind.

So the first thing to do is to build up mindfulness by developing present-moment awareness—that is, by putting energy into the moment. Try to be very silent and maintain that as long as you can throughout the day. The more time you spend in the present moment, the stronger your mindfulness becomes. It's like waking up from sleep in the morning. At first you're a bit dull, but after a while you become aware and energized and you actually know what's going on. Over the course of a retreat, you can watch that morning dullness disappear as your awareness grows. Awareness is there just before you go to sleep, and it's there when you wake up again. It's wonderful to see for yourself that by reducing activity and conversation and increasing meditation, you can sharpen your mindfulness, hour by hour, day by day.

Getting Ready to Watch the Breath

As your mindfulness grows stronger, it's easier to see the bad habits and hindrances that usually lead you by the nose. You clearly see the stupid states of mind that you sometimes get into, like getting angry at other people. When you're not mindful, these habits keep coming up, but when you are mindful, you can see them as they happen. You can see these states arising and their consequences. You can see what they do to you and to others. When you see these habits and know that they cause pain and suffering, you become motivated to stop them.

Not only do you see the problem, but you also see the solution: restraint. Mindfulness makes restraint possible. Without mindfulness you might want to be restrained, but you just can't do it because you're still in the dark. When mindfulness grows, however, the hindrances and defilements are easier to spot. This is the real beginning of your meditation practice.

Ever since I started teaching breath meditation, I've noticed that people tend to begin watching the breath too soon. If you haven't settled down properly and you're not mindful enough, you can only watch the breath through willpower, which is not sustainable for very long. You start watching the breath, and you become dull or even fall asleep, because the mind isn't yet ready. Only when mindfulness attains a certain degree of clarity is it easy to watch the breath, and only then can you truly start the meditation practice.

Having meditated for a long time, I understand my mind well enough to know what it needs. Before anything else, mindfulness must be shined and increased. If it's not the right time, if mindfulness is not sharp enough, I know the mind won't stick with the breath. I have to do more mindfulness practices; I have to wake up and create a bit of joy. I have to get energy and focus silently in the moment. I know that when silence, present-moment awareness, and mindfulness are strong enough, it's easy to watch the breath. I simply tell my mind to watch the breath and it does so with pleasure.

According to the *Ānāpānasati Sutta* (MN 118.17), the first thing a meditator has to do is establish mindfulness as a "priority." This is my favorite translation for the Pali word *parimukha*, which literally means "in front." Giving something priority means giving it the greatest importance. So before you try to watch the breath, make mindfulness the main thing. Give it priority over everything else—just be aware, alert, awake. The whole reason we do body sweeping, body awareness, or walking meditation is to strengthen mindfulness. Once mindfulness reaches a certain level, it will be bright and awake enough to do the job of focusing on a single object.

Overcoming Defilements

Apart from being alert, you need to know where to put your awareness—that is, to learn to watch the right thing at the right time. If watching the breath isn't working, ask yourself *how* you're watching the breath. Sometimes people watch the breath with control and willpower, with expectations and demands, but they don't see that there is a problem with how they're watching the breath—they're watching it in the wrong way.

It's useful to have a framework for how to relate to the hindrances and defilements. In my experience it's helpful to regard the hindrances and defilements as living in the space between the observer and the observed. The hindrances are not in the breath, and they are not in the consciousness—they are just in between. Look at that space and find out how you're watching the breath. See if you are watching it with craving, desire, ill will, restlessness, dullness, or doubt. In the beginning of a meditation, that is more important than watching the breath itself.

When I meditate, I know I have a problem if I see any sign of hindrances and defilements between me and the breath—such as desiring it to be the beautiful breath or wanting a *nimitta*, that beautiful light of a still mind. Mindfulness spots that desire and knows that it's going to cause

a lot of problems; it's going to be contrary to the goal of peace and stillness. As soon as you see that, it's easy to stop.

If you're not happy with the breath, you'll want something that is more
pleasurable: some sort of fantasy or a cup of coffee. If you're not content,
of course your mind is going to wander off somewhere else. So stop that
ill will. Just say, "I've got no ill will toward this breath even though it's a
bit unpleasant. It's okay—that's just its nature." Then leave it alone for a
while. At the beginning of meditation all meditation objects will be a bit
uncomfortable. That's their nature. When you realize that, you can allow
them to be.

Sometimes when you make a natural transition from one meditation
object to the next—say, from the breath to the beautiful breath, or from
the beautiful breath to the *nimitta*—it's not so attractive at first. You
think, "Should I go back to just the ordinary breath?" Sometimes the
beautiful breath is nice and peaceful, but you might get this big bright
light, a *nimitta*, coming up to disturb you. The point is that whenever
there's a transition there's always a little bit of disturbance. You must be
patient enough to allow it to settle down. Even if the meditation object
has an unpleasant aspect to it, if you have enough mindfulness, you can
bypass the discontent and ill will, and instead have kindness, gentleness,
and letting go. In fact, those are the three things that I always try to put
between me and the object.

Meditation Kamma

Practicing in this way, you focus on the space between the observer and
the object, and you put those three things—letting go, kindness, and gentleness, the three aspects of *sammāsaṅkappa*—in that space. You're not
trying to get anything, and you don't have ill will. You're putting gentleness between you and the object, not force or aggression. If you put those
three positive qualities in that space, and you're mindful to make sure they
remain there, the breath becomes smooth and peaceful.

Sometimes I call this practice being mindful of *kamma*, because what
you put between yourself and the object is the *kamma* that you're making

now. If you're watching the object while trying to gain something or get rid of something, you're making disturbing *kamma* that is going to have bad results in the future. But when you put the positive qualities of letting go, kindness, and gentleness between you and the meditation object, you generate the most pure and beautiful *kamma*. It leads to wonderful consequences. This is why you should make peace with every moment and be kind and gentle with every moment, no matter what you're experiencing. Once you're making good *kamma* in this moment, the result is peace—the meditation becomes deep, and you have a wonderful time. The breath becomes peaceful and smooth and the mind becomes beautiful. You achieve this because you're putting attention on how you're aware, not so much on what you're aware of.

Another way of looking at this is to realize that mindfulness needs to be paired with wisdom. In the *suttas* this is known as *sati-sampajañña*. This is the wisdom of knowing the instructions, knowing what to look for, and knowing where to look. It's amazing how combining mindfulness and wisdom increases your ability to develop deep and powerful meditation. Because you're mindful you can see what you're doing, and the wisdom can then stop the negative *kamma* and replace it with positive *kamma*.

When you start meditating you might be tired or restless, but if you make peace with the moment and let go, if you're kind and gentle, you'll find it's easy to watch the breath. Gradually the breath changes. Because you're making good *kamma*, the breath becomes more attractive, stable, and peaceful. And because the breath becomes more still, your mindfulness in turn becomes more energetic and therefore more powerful.

Overcoming the Subtle Defilements

When you develop the power of mindfulness, it's like turning up the lights in your mind. You can see deeper, you can see more, and you're more discerning. As you watch the mind, you can see defilements that are so subtle that you've never seen them before. You can see what stops the breath from turning into the beautiful breath. You can see when you're expecting something or trying too hard. Because these things are habitual—so common for you that you don't normally notice them—you only see them when mindfulness gets powerful. This is how the path of developing *ānāpānasati*—meditation on the breath—leads to the *nimitta* and *jhāna*.

In fact, this is insight meditation. Through mindfulness you get insight into the subtle defilements and the way they work. You see their source and their nature. You understand that the defilements promise you so much but that they never actually deliver. Without insight into these problems, you'll never be able to transcend them and go deeper. But once you see how the mind operates, it becomes easy to handle. Once you have understood the problem, all you need to do is see the defilement and it disappears. This is well expressed in a metaphor from the *suttas*: once you notice Māra, all you need to say is "Māra, I know you," and Māra just slinks off and goes away (e.g., SN 5:1).

There's a process happening here, a whole sequence of causes and effects. As you develop mindfulness, it gets more and more refined, it gets energized, and it can see more. Mindfulness brightens up, and you start to experience joy. That joy in turn affects the way you look at things, and this makes the breath beautiful. And to experience this happy mindfulness and this beautiful breath is what any teacher would want for his disciples.

A happy mindfulness is also a playful mindfulness—it can take an object and turn it around this way and that, and it's fun. So while you're watching the beautiful breath, you have the opportunity to understand it in every which way. Mindfulness becomes powerful and far more penetrating.

The Nimitta Stage

Mindfulness isn't a separate entity—it's bound up with stillness and joy, and obviously with wisdom. It carries with it instructions, and the more powerful mindfulness is, the more clearly it remembers them. It knows what to do because it has been well trained, and it understands the power of stillness. Whenever you move the mind you disturb everything, and you lose energy and depth. Your mindfulness decreases in power and becomes less sharp. But when you remain still—peacefully not doing anything, just being more fully where you already are—mindfulness only keeps increasing. So at this stage the job of mindfulness is not so much to watch the object as to make sure the mind doesn't move.

This is where you get the mindfulness Ajahn Chah refers to in his famous simile of the still forest pool. In that simile Ajahn Chah isn't just watching the animals come out to drink, he's also watching his body so it doesn't move. In the same way, you watch your mind, making sure it doesn't move so a *nimitta* can come out to play. Your mindfulness is focused on stillness, ensuring that your mind doesn't waver. With that degree of mindfulness and power, the *nimitta* remains steady, and you see how it's done. You don't react. You don't get afraid or excited.

Now you're getting into the really beautiful parts of meditation—sharp mindfulness and powerful bliss. But there's more to these states than just enjoyment. There's a sense that incredibly profound things are happening here. After you emerge from one of these states—even the *nimitta* stage, let alone *jhāna*—mindfulness has been further empowered. You're not sleepy at all, nor can you get argumentative; you see deeply and powerfully all around you. It's amazing how acutely you feel your body—you sense any tension, tightness, sickness, or pain. When you do body awareness with that degree of mindfulness, you just zap things out of existence. It's not that you have some sort of superhuman power; it's just the nature of mindfulness at this stage. You can warm, ease, soothe, heal, or do whatever you want with your body. That's how much power mindfulness has when you come out of the *nimitta* stage.

Your mindfulness is so strong and still that you can focus on any object and stay there. If you really want to develop some understanding of the nature of your body or anything else, the time to do it is after a deep meditation. Anyone who has experienced deep meditation understands why it is necessary for the gaining of real wisdom. If the mindfulness prior to such meditation is like a spoon, the mindfulness after deep meditation is an earth mover. If you want to dig a big hole—that is, if you want to acquire deep wisdom—the only option is the earth mover. At this stage of mindfulness, your power and penetration are that much greater.

The joy of such deep meditation is the happiness available in monastic life or on retreats. It's great to develop it, and there's no reason why you can't; you just have to develop mindfulness and meditation stage by stage. If you have never experienced these things and all you can see is the bottom of the ladder, it can be dispiriting when someone describes the top—you don't know what's in between or how to get there. But as you proceed, you know, "I can do the first stage; I can do the second stage; I can do the third stage." You actually see the rungs on the ladder, and you know you can reach these stages. You know it can be done and how to do it, and you're developing motivation and mindfulness together.

The Fruits of Mindfulness

So you should give prominence to the practice of mindfulness. It's an important part of a retreat, and the beginning of the retreat is the time to develop it. It's worthwhile to put in the care and the effort. As you proceed, you wake up more and more and build up energy and discernment. You see the problems and you solve them. You become more peaceful, still, wise, and happy. And meditation gradually gets easier and easier.

Because present-moment awareness and silence are important foundations for strengthening mindfulness, remember to develop them throughout the day. When doing walking meditation, be aware of this end of the path, the other end of the path, and the middle of the path. When you're eating or talking or whatever else you're doing, make mindfulness important.

Put mindfulness in the space between you—the observer—and whatever you're experiencing—whatever you're watching and whatever your meditation object is—because that's where the action is. When mindfulness is strong enough, you can get rid of the grosser defilements. When the grosser defilements are gone, mindfulness will increase, and you will be able to see the more subtle defilements. When the more subtle defilements go, mindfulness will get even stronger. Then you will be able to get rid of the most subtle of defilements. When you overcome even these, you're free and the path is clear. You can watch the breath become very peaceful, still, and smooth, and your meditation is simply wonderful. You can sit for hours and really surprise yourself with how deep you can go, and you marvel at how peaceful and beautiful it all is.

You're on the path. When mindfulness gets very, very strong, who knows what will happen? You may even be able to see the deepest *Dhamma* of all—that is, nonself and the four noble truths. Maybe you can end suffering during your next retreat!

Medicines for the Mind 4

THE PRACTICE OF MEDITATION is a well-worn path for calming the mind and bringing it into a state of peace, power, and happiness. This practice has been going on for such a long time that any problem you may be having now has already been faced and overcome by many others in the past. What's important is how we remember the strategies for overcoming those obstacles and our motivation and diligence in putting them into place—that is, how we employ the medicines that cure the diseases of the mind.

Boredom

One of the major problems that can arise during a long retreat is boredom. When I was a young monk in Thailand, we would often complain that there were too many things going on. There was too much work, too many people, too many ceremonies, too much morning chanting, too much evening chanting. I would sometimes fantasize about being in a monastery where there were no meetings and where you hardly had any work to do so you could sit and walk all day. I fantasized about such monasteries, but of course, you get bored and restless in a place like that! You suffer a lot, and your fantasy turns around: "If I could only find a monastery where there was work or something to do. Maybe I could talk to someone, or at least take part in some chanting and group meditation in the evening." But this is missing the whole point, because the standard in the *suttas* and in the forest tradition is to spend lots of time in solitude, to have little work and little contact with others. Those of you who have investigated the teachings of the Buddha in the *suttas* and the *vinaya* know that seclusion is important. I try my hardest to arrange my monastery to give the maximum possible seclusion and the fewest number of meetings. Of course, the result may be the arising of boredom, restlessness, and fantasies, or getting fed up with your own company. Nevertheless, it's worth facing those obstacles and finding the strategies to overcome them.

You should investigate boredom. Where does it come from? Often boredom arises during a transition from being busy to being settled. Some young people who come to a retreat or a monastery get bored because there are no televisions or iPods. There isn't much to entertain you. When you look at boredom you see that it's a reaction to relative levels of busyness: it arises because of the difference between your previous level of activity and what you're facing now. What's exciting in a monastery—like having toast in the morning—would seem boring to most people in the world. They would think, "What's the big deal? Is that all you guys fantasize about?" What's actually happening is that the mind isn't used to dealing with the subtle and peaceful states that result from reduced activity. It hasn't adjusted to the lack of stimulation, and it needs time to settle down.

Although moving from activity to less activity may make you bored at first, after a while you start to wake up to the interesting aspects of that lifestyle, to the joy and delight of being alone and not having much to do. It's like going from a lit room into a dark room. At first you can't see. It takes a while for your eyes to adjust to the darkness; only then can you see the shapes of things. In the same way, when you go from activity to less activity, it takes time for the mind to adjust to the lessening of sensory stimulation. After a while it does adapt, and what was once boring and uninteresting, with little to attract the mind, starts to become beautiful and delightful.

So the first strategy when you are bored is to be patient with that boredom. Leave it alone. Don't try to fill that hole of boredom with activity. If you do, you're just stimulating the mind again. It's like going outside at night and turning on a light—you miss the experience of the more subtle shapes in the darkness. Recently I went to a social gathering with the famous scientist Sir Roger Penrose where part of the program was to look through telescopes. It happened to be a clear night, so we could actually see things like Jupiter and its moons. But when we first went into the observatory, we had to wait for a few moments after the lights were turned off to let our eyes get accustomed to the starlight. It was just a case of waiting a while, and then we were able to see the beautiful stars in the sky. In the same way, you need to dim the sensory activity if you want to see the beautiful stars in the mind. I'm not only talking about the *nimitta* here, but also the subtle, peaceful, beautiful happiness that occurs when the five senses are subdued.

So when you calm down the senses of seeing, hearing, smelling, tasting, and touching, it's quite common to go through that stage of boredom. When the lights are turned off and you can't see, there's nothing to grab your attention. What's important here is to be patient and have faith that the mind will soon begin to see things that are very interesting, if you can only manage to stay with the boredom. People who go to an art gallery or listen to fine music may get bored if they expect something more exciting like a blockbuster movie or Jimi Hendrix. But after a while, if they can calm down that excitement of the senses, they get the chance to savor things that are far more delightful. So stay with the boredom, don't interrupt the process, and after a while the boredom turns into something beautiful. The mind opens up to a more subtle mental landscape, and you start to appreciate what can happen in solitude. But you need patience, because sometimes it does take a long time.

Restlessness

Another common problem is restlessness. You don't want to sit still, the body is uncomfortable, or the mind just won't stay with the breath or any other meditation object you're trying to focus on. This happens when you use too much force. Sometimes the best thing to do is just to be patient and wait—to allow the restlessness to be rather than try to control it.

One of the great strategies I often talk about is the one I call "the water buffalo mind." This strategy is named after an incident that occurred just outside Wat Pah Nanachat in Thailand when Ajahn Jagaro was the abbot and I was the second monk. Early one morning when I had already gone on almsround but Ajahn Jagaro was still in the monastery, a man came running into the monastery with half his finger missing. He had been taking his water buffalo out to graze when the water buffalo got scared and tried to run away. The rope holding the water buffalo was wound around the man's finger, and when he tried to hold the water buffalo back, the rope tore half his finger off. Of course, it was a very bloody finger, so Ajahn Jagaro immediately got a car and took the man to the hospital. I saw him a couple of days later with bandages on and then later with only half a finger. This happened because he didn't know how to deal with a restless water buffalo. He should have just let it go.

You should use the same strategy when the mind is restless—just let it go. Don't try to hold it back. If you try to stop or control it, the mind just gets more wanton and more difficult. All you need to do is say, "Okay mind, if that's what you want to do, off you go." Your job is just to be mindful and at peace and watch where this silly old mind wants to go. Your job is not to stop the mind, but to watch it, understand it, and be kind and gentle with it.

It's as if you're dealing with a little child who wants to run this way and that. Sometimes young children come to our monastery, and often they're very noisy. If you've had a nice meditation, the screaming of those children really pierces your mind, and it's quite unpleasant. But it's their nature to do things like that; you can't expect kids to do anything different. In the same way, it's the nature of the mind to be restless.

So please don't feel guilty if your mind is restless. What's happening is not yours, it's not a "me," and it's not a problem; it's just the nature of things, arising according to *kammic* causes from the past. You can't go into the past and cancel out those causes; you're stuck with their results right now. If the mind wants to run off, the only thing to do is to remember the *sammāsaṅkappa*, right intention: just let it go, and be kind and gentle with it.

These beautiful teachings of the Buddha are straight to the point—they show you that your attitude toward what's happening is the most important part of meditation. So let that water buffalo of a mind run off. If you do, you'll find that the water buffalo doesn't run very far before it settles down and waits for its owner. It's part of the family. It likes staying with its owner. So you only need to follow it for a short distance. It's a bit of extra exercise, but that's much better than having your finger torn off. Then you can grab the rope again and gently lead the water buffalo to where you wanted to take it in the first place. Maybe you've lost a little bit of time, but at least you don't have to go to the hospital. In the same way, when your mind gets restless—when it gets crazy and wants to do all sorts of stupid things—your job is to let it go with kindness and gentleness.

Forcing the mind is wrong, but so is indulgence. Both force and indulgence actually feed that water buffalo mind. By indulgence I mean turning your mind toward sensuality, thinking about sex, the future, movies, or music, or whatever else you think about when you're restless. If you keep on leaning in that direction, of course the mind will keep going that way. But if you stand back with equanimity—if you let go, if you're kind and gentle—that water buffalo mind soon stops. Dealing with restlessness doesn't need to be a battle. If it becomes a battle—perhaps getting even worse—it's because you're feeding it with negativity, guilt, or indulgence. You're not really facing it in the proper way. Instead of just allowing the old *kamma* to ripen, you're making new bad *kamma*.

Be a Passive Observer

When you're restless just be at peace with it. Regard yourself as the passenger, not the driver. Being the driver means you're driving the restless mind; being the passenger means you're sitting in the back, not involved at all, just observing where the journey takes you. This idea of non-involvement and disengagement is one of the beautiful attitudes that I use in my meditation. You disengage from things so that all you do is watch your mind. When it does this or thinks that, it's as if you're standing back and watching it from a distance. The best metaphor for such disengagement is sitting in the cinema. In the cinema people sometimes get so involved in the movie that they start to cry or get excited or scared. Why do they do that? As long as you can stand back and remember that these are just causes and conditions rolling on—not me, not mine, not a self, nothing to do with me—then you won't get involved. You can watch restlessness or boredom or whatever else with a feeling of disengagement. You're just knowing, and "the knower" is coming into focus.

The knower is like the patron in the movie theater, just watching the movie play out on the screen, always remembering that "the one who knows" is not involved in any of this. Use this idea of the knower—not mistaking it for a permanent self—as a steppingstone to peace. Imagine yourself sitting inside yourself. If you do that, you get a sense of detachment from what's happening, and that detachment leads to a kind and gentle letting go. So whenever there's involvement, whenever your meditation is not going well or you're feeling fed up with it—whenever there's that sense of me doing something—remember the attitude of watching a movie. There's no need to get excited or disappointed, no need to cry or be afraid; it's only a movie.

To illustrate this point, I like to use the story of the drive-in movie theater in Jamaica that had a screen made of concrete one foot thick. The patrons of that cinema loved cowboy and Indian westerns, especially the gunfights. Whenever there was a gunfight on the screen, they would get out their own guns and join in. Can you imagine that? It makes me smile even now, thinking of all these guys sitting on the ground or in their convertibles, waiting for a gunfight scene so they could take part. Wouldn't it be good fun? The owner of the movie theater went through so many cloth screens that he decided the only way to keep his business going was to erect a concrete screen.

You can see why I bring this up. People get involved, and they want to shoot the sheriff, the cowboy, or the Indian. You want to shoot the restless mind, to destroy the boredom or otherwise get involved in this or that. We get attached and involved and create more problems for ourselves. Patience is when we stop and say, "It'll work itself out. The water buffalo will run off, but eventually it will stop."

Always remember that it's just a movie playing—just the result of the five *khandhas* and the six sense bases doing their thing, all according to cause and effect. There's nothing substantial you should be worried about. That's the reason you can disengage. This is one of the best antidotes to restlessness I know, because when I disengage and just watch all this stuff come and go, I cut off its source of fuel. I understand that restlessness is caused by something, and that something is me getting involved in the whole process. As soon as I stop driving the process and take away the engagement—imagining myself as a person sitting in a movie theater just watching—the mind starts to calm down and get quiet. Restlessness fades, boredom disappears, and the quietness, gentleness, and stillness of meditation start to take over.

Tiredness and Energy

Another common problem faced during meditation is dullness and sleepiness. Please remember never to fight that tiredness. I say that from bitter experience: I was encouraged to do that, and I found it completely counterproductive. Every time you fight tiredness, you just get tense, since fighting leads you in the opposite direction of gentleness, kindness, and letting go. It's actually a subtle form of ill will.

Some meditators feel embarrassed or guilty when they're tired. We feel humiliated by the fact that we've been meditating for many years and still can't keep a straight back early in the morning. But guilt just adds to the sense of ego and self, and we start to own these problems. Be careful not to own your sleepiness—it has nothing to do with you; it's just an effect stemming from a cause, that's all. If you get sleepy, just stay with it—watch it, be kind and gentle with it, investigate it. What does it feel like? How long does it last? And most importantly, what causes it and what sorts of things make it fade away? After it fades away, what's left? It's not just about getting rid of sleepiness at all costs; it's about overcoming it in a wise way so that your meditation can take off.

Of course sleepiness can be overcome if you force the mind. You can meditate on the edge of a precipice or—as we used to do in Thailand—

put a matchbox on the top of your head, or pins under your hands, or get somebody to stand behind you with a stick to beat you if you start nodding your head even slightly. You certainly won't doze off, but the result is fear and tension. You're just getting rid of one defilement and replacing it with another.

Instead be patient with that sleepiness and tiredness; let it be and disengage. It's as if you're sitting in the movie theater again, and this time there's something wrong with the projector. The picture isn't clear; it's out of focus. But it doesn't matter; it's not your problem. The proprietor of the movie theater will fix it up. You just leave it alone and sit there with patience. If you really have patience, after a while the tiredness just vanishes, like mist when the sun comes up. Patience is all that's required. This non-doing allows the mind to become energized. Remember this little bit of mental science: when the energy stops going into the doing it will start to flow into the knowing.

The trouble is that a lot of the time you don't have enough confidence to just be with the tiredness. Instead you keep pushing it along by getting involved. Because you're trying to fix the problem, you get even more tired, and you create more problems for yourself. But when you see the truth of that simple statement—that when the energy stops going into the doing it starts to flow into the knowing—then you know why you get tired initially, and you know what happens if you are patient and do nothing. That understanding should give you a lot of confidence.

So just imagine yourself watching all of this, not moving from your seat, not shouting at the movie, not getting your gun out and shooting at the tiredness because you don't like it. When you just sit and watch—even with dullness—you can see that the energy eventually goes into mindfulness. The mind brightens up. When you understand the whole process, meditation is much easier and much more fun. Once you know how it all works, you know how you make mistakes and how you can become peaceful and joyful and increase your energy. This becomes a wonderful way of calming the *saṅkhāras*, the mental activity, the will, the controlling.

To help the process along, try contemplating nonself. Just say, "There's no one to control this anyway; there's nobody in here; it's not my business; let's just leave it alone." This is true Buddhism; it's exactly what the *suttas* say. Understand that there's no "you" here to do anything—it's just the five *khandhas*—so why struggle? That sort of reflection may be enough to give you the confidence to leave things alone and to help you know what leaving things alone truly means.

Overcoming Desire and Ill Will

Of the five hindrances, the first two, desire and ill will, are the most important. Desire means wanting something other than what you already have; ill will means not wanting what you do have. So they're both just forms of wanting. And when you want something different—whether it's the next level of meditation, food, the end of a retreat, or whatever else—it always takes you away from where you are.

In Greek mythology there are beings known as sirens. These creatures draw unwary sailors onto the rocks with their enticing songs. This is what desires do: they entice you, pull you in the direction of the desired object, and shipwreck your meditation. You get no happiness or peace. Desires pull you away from where you can find true satisfaction. So instead of allowing yourself to be pulled along, remember that fulfilling your endless desires is not in your power. Just sit there. You don't move; you just watch.

Just as desire creates doing, so does ill will. Desire and ill will are what make you move, what make you tired. They create the activity of the mind that disturbs and agitates you. Once you see ill will and desire and how they work, you can say, "No, I'm not going to get involved in that anymore; what I have is good enough."

"Good enough"—*por dee* in Thai—is a beautiful mantra. It's great to use in your meditation no matter what you're experiencing. If you're so tired that your head is almost on the floor, say, "This is good enough." As you breathe in and out, say, "Good enough." But you have to be consistent and make every moment good enough. In this way you subdue the desires that take you away and the ill will that keeps you from staying here, and you get a sense of stillness and satisfaction. There's nothing you need, nothing you desire, and the here and now really is good enough.

You now start to recognize and experience the delight of meditation, the delight born of being still and wanting nothing. You see that the "good enough" practice is just the beginning. When you convince yourself that the present moment is good enough and you stay with what you have, it's not just good enough anymore: it's actually damned good and immensely beautiful. No matter where you start, when you stay with what you have, it grows in beauty, delight, and profundity.

Many years ago I developed the simile of the lotus flower with a thousand petals. It doesn't matter what sort of lotus you begin with. Even the most unpromising, dirty, straggly, malformed lotus will do, because inside every lotus there's a beautiful heart. What I mean is that every experience you have—this one right now, or even the worst one you've had during a long retreat—becomes delightful if you can only stay with it. Don't change it, move it, or try to get rid of it. Don't have desire for it or ill will toward it. Be with whatever is there—even pain, boredom, or desperation. Even the lotus that is all black and dirty and ugly outside opens up and becomes delightful if you just stay with it. The more you stay with it, the more it opens up. The more you say, "good enough," the more those ugly outer petals open up to reveal less ugly petals. Then the less ugly petals open up to fine petals, and soon you get into the beautiful stuff.

It's extremely useful to know that this is the way the mind works. It doesn't matter what you're experiencing, or what you start off with—anything can be transformed. You don't have to get rid of all the problems and then start meditation afterward. Start with your problem; be with it and allow it to be. This is good enough. If you don't move, if you have no desire or ill will, you find that your mind bores into the problem, opens it up, and what was once intolerable is now easily endured. Next it becomes quite nice, and having become quite nice, it then becomes delightful. And it all started out from the most unpromising of beginnings. So whatever you're experiencing, know that it's good enough. In this way, you are abandoning many of the obstacles to meditation.

The worst problem in meditation is ill will—saying, "I don't like this," and always comparing and being negative. This kind of fault-finding should be abandoned by developing its opposite—accepting, embracing, and looking for the delight and beauty in things. This is actually quite easy. Just look at the natural beauty around you. In Australia, you can go and find a kangaroo and look at the joey poking its head out of the pouch or watch it jumping up and down. Watch the rain dripping from the edge of the leaves, or go out and look at the stars. There's so much beauty in nature. If you look for that beauty, that delight, you'll get into the habit of not being a fault-finder. Since you're used to seeing the beauty in things, whatever you thought was ugly in your meditation starts to look nice—even beautiful. Beauty is in the eye of the beholder, as they say, and success in meditation is in the attitude of the meditator. If you get that attitude right, it leads to kindness, gentleness, and letting go. You become kind to all things.

It's just like a mother who loves her children even if they're little monsters. You can see the mother cradling her baby and looking after it, and even though it climbs all over her back and half strangles her, the mother still loves that kid. If a mother can love like that, surely you can love your mind! Even though it's a little bit delinquent sometimes, you accept it as good enough.

Ask yourself whether you're being demanding in your meditation. Are you thinking, "I'd better get into *jhāna* on this retreat or get a *nimitta* or at least get peaceful"? If you're demanding, your meditation won't go anywhere. However, if you reduce your demands, it becomes easy to achieve the "good enough" attitude. If you don't make great demands on yourself, life, or the world, it's easier to appreciate them. As it says in the *Mettā Sutta* (Sn. 144), you're "not demanding in nature"; rather, you're "contented and easily satisfied." Train your mind like that. Be contented and build up that contentment; be easily satisfied and then you're heading for *jhāna*.

You don't get the *jhānas* when you want them; they occur only when you build up the causes for their arising. The main cause is stillness of the mind, maintained over long periods of time. The energy pours into pure knowing, and then the mind goes deep into that lotus, and it opens up stage by stage—not according to your timeline, not when you want it to, but according to its own natural schedule. It happens because you're still, and you're still because you're content with little, easily satisfied, and not demanding anything. If you do that in daily life, you're building up the causes for deep meditation.

When you aren't easily satisfied, when you're demanding and full of wants, you also get restless. When you don't get what you want, your desires grow, and you get into a terrible cycle of wanting. You know what it's like sometimes when you're desperate: you don't want to walk, you don't want to sit down, you don't want to sleep, and you think, "I've got nothing I want to do, and whatever I am doing now, I don't want that either." It's a terrible situation to be in when nothing whatsoever satisfies you. It happens because you've developed it, because you've created the causes with wrong attitudes and misdirected attention. But if you develop stillness and calm by being easily satisfied and content, you're creating the causes for powerful meditation to happen. If you just sit there, content, still, and accepting that this is good enough, everything starts to happen. You think, "Wow, at last I can do this!"

Allowing the "You" to Disappear

Always remember that it's not that you can do it; it's that you aren't getting in the way. The process happens when "you" disappear. When you're demanding, you are there. When you have ill will, you are there. When you have craving, you are there. When you have boredom, you are there. All these things create a sense of self that thinks it owns things and gets involved. You are the problem. And you can't just go somewhere else: wherever you go, you take you with you. So everyone should disrobe: take off that "I-garment." That which you take yourself to be, that sense of self, should leave and vanish. When the sense of you disappears, there's no ill will or desire, because they're part of the ego and the illusion of self. Then there can only be contentment and peace.

When I was a kid I was a Cub Scout. We used to get all these badges for things: a badge for being able to make a cup of tea, a badge for being able to light a fire. That's what many people do on retreats—they want a badge for getting *jhāna*, a badge for becoming a stream-winner. But there are no badges on the Buddhist path. On the contrary, we're trying to get rid of all those badges—whatever it is we think we are—so we can just disappear. When you're restless, just disappear; when you're tired, just disappear. When you disappear, everything becomes nice and peaceful. When you're bored, ask, "Who's being bored anyway?" Just disappear and the boredom will vanish.

Be Patient

If you're contented and easily satisfied and have the attitude that the here and now is good enough, then problems occur only at the beginning of the path. After a while, they just vanish, and you're flying—getting into nice meditation and spending hours perfectly happy and content. If that's not happening yet, be patient—it will. It doesn't matter how many years you've been practicing. Even for some of the Buddha's greatest disciples, such as the venerable Anuruddha, it took many, many years before they got the full results of the practice. Give it time. In the *suttas*, when they say that someone from a good family went forth and "in no long time" became an *arahant*, sometimes they mean several decades. Fifteen or twenty years is "no long time" when you consider the timescales of *saṃsāra*.

So don't expect things to happen immediately. Your job is just to be quiet, calm, still, and peaceful. Don't hold on to that water buffalo. Don't chase it. Develop letting go, develop contentment, and develop the "good enough" attitude. By doing these things you're developing the tools to perfect your meditation.

Sometimes a particular attitude or tool you've been using may start to lose its effectiveness. So use another tool, and then another. Little by little, using various strategies, you get through the early difficulties. Once the mind develops properly and you start to experience peace and happiness, you really get into meditation. By then you don't need all that much help. Sure I could give you a few instructions, but you're already off having a wonderful time. And that's exactly what I want for you.

Wisdom Power 5

❖ ❖ ❖

IN ONE OF MY FAVORITE VERSES in the *Dhammapada*, it says, "There is no *jhāna* without wisdom" (verse 372). The verse is about using your faculty of wisdom and insight to develop the deeper stages of meditation. Instead of talking about the wisdom that arises *from* meditation, I want to talk about applying wisdom to the practice of meditation itself. Wisdom can be a powerful tool to help us find the peace, calm, and stillness that take the mind to deeper and deeper levels, eventually allowing us to see the truths of enlightenment.

Letting Go by Understanding Suffering

When people meditate they often use too much force; they just keep bashing away at the same place. Lack of progress isn't always due to insufficient effort or motivation, or too little time spent on the meditation cushion or the walking path. Sometimes it's just that the wisdom isn't sharp enough to get through the problems, and if you only had a bit more wisdom, you would suffer less and achieve deeper states more quickly. Thus cultivating the faculty of wisdom is extremely important.

The first of the four noble truths as expounded in the *Dhamma-cakkappavattana Sutta* is the truth of suffering (SN 56:11). You have to focus your wisdom faculty on that suffering. Suffering just *is*; it has nothing to do with whether or not you're trying to avoid it. Suffering is the nature of the world, the nature of the body, and the nature of the mind. Things don't always go the way you want them to. Occasionally they do, but never as often as you'd like. The suffering that comes from being frustrated with meditation practice—being bored or feeling stuck or whatever—is an aspect of the first noble truth. Disappointments, not getting what you want in life—basically the five *khandhas*—this is all suffering. So don't force the issue and say, "This isn't right; it shouldn't be this way; I'm doing something wrong." Instead, stop, focus, and remind yourself that this is just the nature of things. If meditation doesn't go the way you want it to, or if the body is aching or the mind is sleepy, remember: that's just the nature of the body and the mind.

A wonderful thing happens when you get wise to the nature of the body, the mind, and life itself. When you realize that it's all just nature, just a process of cause and effect, you also realize that it's not your problem anymore. You see that detachment comes from the wisdom of recognizing the nature of suffering in life: you can't do much about it, so you leave it alone. When you leave it alone, you develop the mental attitude that is aware and alert, that watches but doesn't get involved. If you don't arouse the doer in the difficult moments, you're actually turning a bad meditation into a source of future calm. In fact, the whole job of meditation practice is putting effort into how you're experiencing things, not worrying about what you're experiencing. Focus on how you're aware of the hindrances, the desire and ill will, the boredom and frustration. What's important is your attitude toward the situations you come across in meditation and how you react to them, rather than the situations themselves.

To establish the right attitude, we need to use our wisdom. When we realize that our experiences are just nature, we don't react by feeling afraid, guilty, frustrated, or disappointed. We don't lose our confidence, thinking, "I can't do it." Of course you can't *do* it! I can't do meditation either. Every time Ajahn Brahm starts to meditate, he messes it up. But I've got enough wisdom to know that if I step out of the way, a beautiful, clear space appears between me and what I'm watching. Then there's no frustration or boredom. If those feelings still linger in the background, you just leave them alone. You don't get involved or create more problems. You just watch and gather the data.

Observe and Learn

If you're having problems with a wandering mind or a sleepy mind, remember that such negative states arise only to provide an escape from suffering. Because you're not excited or entertained, meditation can seem dull or even boring. Your habit is to escape. We all have our escape strategies. But remember: when you use those escapes, you're not learning anymore; you're just wasting time.

It's important to observe your reactions to things. This practice is wise in itself, and it develops further wisdom; it helps you go far deeper in your meditation. Whenever anything comes up that is unsatisfactory—that's when you observe. You may be bored, frustrated, or tired, and nothing seems to work. You don't know what you're going to do—you can't stay in your room, you don't want to do walking meditation, and you've got nothing to read. That's great—just observe your reactions to this unpleasantness. In other words, this is the perfect time to just watch without reacting. You observe and gather data, because you want to understand. When you gather data, you start to learn from your experiences. The very fact that you're accepting these experiences is grist for the mill. Here is the data for insight, the dung for your garden.

When you simply accept your experiences—whatever they are—you find that not only do you learn from them, but suddenly you're free from them. You're not trying to control them anymore, because you realize you don't own them. So if you get bored, don't own your boredom. If you get frustrated, don't own your frustration. Whatever is happening is just a process of cause and effect, the coming and going of mental and physical phenomena. Use your insight and your understanding of the *Dhamma* to know that this is suffering—what else did you expect? If you think you're going to eliminate it by coming to a monastery or a retreat, then you've come to the wrong place. You don't escape from suffering on a retreat; you face it and disengage from it. So there is a way out, but it's an indirect one. It's when you don't desire to escape that the escape happens.

Investigate and Understand

Wherever you go, wherever you travel, whatever happens in your life, you should know that a change in circumstances never eliminates the suffering. Wherever you go, the problems will always be there with you. This is the nature of life, the play of the five *khandhas*, and it's nothing you can control. Sometimes the body is sick, sometimes it's tired. Now you're happy, now you're unhappy. That's just the world of feeling—you cannot get complete, utter, unchanging happiness. You may think, "One day I'll get into *jhāna*, and then I'll be happy." Yes, it's nice when you get into *jhāna*, but then you come out afterward, and the bliss is all gone. Whatever you do, even if you experience *jhāna*, it's not the end of suffering. But if you keep watching, insight will arise. The mind learns more about the real problems and how they can be overcome. So whatever you experience in life, just stay with it.

One helpful thing about a retreat is the lack of escapes. Because there are few escapes, it's more difficult to run away from the problems that arise. When they do arise, see them as opportunities for investigation. A useful technique is to associate every emotional quality with its corresponding physical feeling. If you're really bored, there's something in your body that you associate with boredom, some sort of feeling. So investigate the physical feeling to understand these emotional states.

If you get bored, ask yourself, "What is boredom?" Investigate it. Don't try to escape from it—try to understand it; face it squarely. If you get frustrated, ask, "What is frustration? What does frustration feel like?" Be with it for a long, long time, until you know it thoroughly. When you do, you become free from it. When meditation is frustrating or boring, instead of making more bad *kamma*—which leads to the obstacle appearing again and again—just understand it and you can let it go. You understand that this is nature, just like when rain clouds appear in the sky: here they come; it's the season for rain; there they go again. It's sunny and then it's dark; the moon comes out or it doesn't. When you understand that this has nothing to do with you, that it's just nature, then you let go and get a sense of distance and freedom from what you're experiencing.

When you're too close to what you're experiencing, you end up owning it—and that's when you become it. When the "I" starts to get involved, there's a problem. You need to develop detachment. You need to understand that it's not "*my* suffering" or "*my* boredom." When you investigate, you come to see that all these things are naturally occurring qualities that cannot be controlled. For example, when you're bored, it's often because the mind isn't soft enough to appreciate the subtle aspects of meditation. If you get sleepy, it might be that mindfulness is not sharp enough to see the beauty of the quiet, peaceful mind. Frustration arises because you're impatient or because you think you can control your experiences, and then you get disappointed when they don't go your way. But when you realize that these things occur naturally and that there's no controller here, how can frustration ever occur?

Consider the simile of the driverless bus. Your life is like a bus with nobody in the driver's seat—that's what the *suttas* and all the great teachers tell us, and it's also what I say. When you realize there's no one driving the bus, all you can do is sit down in your seat and stop complaining. Since there's no driver, there's no one to shout at to hurry up and get out of here or ask to slow down because you want to enjoy the ride. You go through ugly territory, nice territory, and beautiful territory, and you're at peace with all of it. Every time you try to shout at the driver, you're not attending to what you're really experiencing or learning from it. You're getting involved rather than detaching; owning things rather than letting go; trying to make things happen rather than letting them be.

It's the same with meditation practice. Once you recognize that, meditation becomes incredibly easy. Meditation really is an easy thing to do, but most people just don't get it. What they do is try harder to make it easy—but that's a self-contradiction. You try to make it easy, but the more you try, the harder it becomes. The reason you try harder is because you're not getting the results you expect. Rather than trying harder, you should be mindful, investigate, and learn. Use that as your "trying." So put aside the effort, let go of the struggle, and instead investigate and allow your understanding to grow. What does it feel like physically and emotionally? How long does it last?

You can try Ajahn Chah's method: when you get angry, put a clock in front of you and see how long you can be angry. Next time you're bored, see how long you can be bored. Keep a diary of your boring moments and see if you can beat your own record. Compare it with your friends and see who can be bored the longest. Give a prize to the most bored person! Whatever you encounter, don't run away. Facing these little demons— these negative states of mind—is much more effective than you imagine. You face them, and it's as if they fade away and disappear. I often say that if you see a ghost, face the ghost nose to nose and say "boo." The ghost will run a mile; it's more scared of you than you are of it.

When you face the demons in the mind and they disappear, you've gotten through something and you've understood it. You're getting wiser, and that wisdom helps you the next time you meditate. You know exactly what's happening, how the mind works, and how to overcome these bad habits of the mind, these echoes of the past.

Replace Willpower with Wisdom Power

It's very difficult to encourage and inspire people without also frustrating them. You want to describe the fruits of the practice—profound experiences like a *nimitta*, *jhāna*, and stream-winning—to give people some inspiration. It's like a travel agent telling you how nice it's going to be when you get to the Jhāna Hotel in this great resort called Nibbāna. But people often look at those things and take them as goals to be achieved. They feel inadequate to the task and then experience frustration instead of inspiration. For this reason, it's important to describe not just the goal and some of the beautiful experiences you can expect along the way but also the obstacles to getting there.

So when frustration, boredom, or anger come up, don't struggle—just stay with whatever it is and then see what happens. When you're bored or frustrated, you're in the manure. When you learn to step out of it, you're experiencing a detached attitude of objectivity. When you see the obstacles from a distance, you can understand why I call them "fertilizer." You can't expect to have a great meditation every day, but you can always create the causes for having one tomorrow: just watch, and don't get involved. You know it's a tough day today, but you just allow it to be. Let the energy flow into just knowing, into passive awareness. Take it away from the controller, the arguer, the reactive mind.

The more you allow passive awareness to develop and just endure things without reacting to them, the more energy goes into mindfulness. Stand back: don't grab hold of things, and don't try to push them away. Allow things to be, as you do with the clouds in the sky. In this way you're channeling energy into mindfulness, into knowing, and all those negative states of mind just vanish. The mind becomes energized, and meditation feels easy. The more you react negatively to yourself or others, and the more you struggle, the deeper you get into a mess. It's like stepping into quicksand—the more you panic and struggle, the deeper in you go. In the same way, if you panic and struggle in the difficult moments of meditation, you sink into the quicksand of those negative states. So just allow things to be, be patient, and use the experience as an opportunity to develop wisdom. When the wisdom starts to bite, the problem just disappears.

When you start using wisdom power rather than willpower, not only do you get rid of the difficult problems and the negative states of mind, but you have more energy, and you know how to take meditation to a deeper level. You know what the present moment is, and you know that the reason the mind wanders off is fault-finding, saying, "The present moment isn't good enough; I want it to be better." If you have expectations due to the good meditations you've had in the past, thinking, "Now it's getting close; here it comes!"—you've already blown it. When you see this through your own investigation, it's easy to just leave things alone.

The point of meditation isn't to get a *nimitta* or *jhāna*—it's to create the causes for a *nimitta* and *jhāna* to arise by themselves and to create the causes for the enlightenment experiences that follow. Our whole focus is on creating the causes for these things, and that becomes our wisdom power. The causes for these things are letting go, kindness, and gentleness—in short, *sammāsaṅkappa*. You give all of your energy, body, and mind, just for this moment. You let go and you give up, expecting nothing in return. Always remember not to look for results in your meditation. If you try to get something out of it, all you get is suffering. You're meditating to let go, to give up—you have no expectations whatsoever.

Letting go, *paṭinissagga*, means giving and expecting nothing in return. We don't meditate to gain badges or attainments. We're not trying to get something that we can go and tell our friends about: "I did a retreat with Ajahn Brahm and I got this and I got that." We're trying to abandon our defilements; we're meditating for freedom.

Be Content with the Present Moment

Some years ago I was in Japan and my hosts put me up in a five-star hotel. They had forgotten that they should feed a Theravada monk before midday. By the time we got to a certain high-class restaurant, it was just after noon. I refused to eat, which meant I didn't eat at all that day. I was tired and I just wanted to be quiet and meditate, but it was a noisy hotel. I ended up sitting in this room that people pay a fortune to stay in, thinking, "I'm in a prison." I was in prison in a five-star hotel because I didn't want to be there. I soon realized what I was doing and put a stop to that stupid state of mind. But the point is that you can be in prison in a five-star hotel or on a sunny beach. It doesn't really matter where you are; any place you don't want to be is a prison.

So when you're meditating, ask yourself, "Do I want to be here in this moment, or do I want to be somewhere else?" If you want to be somewhere else, you'll never be peaceful or get into deep meditation. But if you stop yourself, wisdom will tell you, "No, this is good enough. I want to be here in this moment, with my aching legs, my itchy nose, in this noisy hut, with my stupid mind—I want to be just here." When you want to be exactly where you happen to be, you're free.

I know of a monk who was put in jail in Thailand many years ago. He was innocent. He was sent to jail when he was about to become the *Sangharaja*, the head of the monastic hierarchy in Thailand, because some other monk who wanted that position accused him of being a communist. He was in jail for two years, during which time he wrote his biography. He loved that time in jail. He didn't have to give any talks, nor speak to people after meals. He had clean, simple food and a nice little room for himself. He said it was wonderful to have so much freedom. If you *want* to be in the prison cell, you're free.

That was a deep, powerful wisdom teaching for me. I realized that it doesn't matter what I'm doing or where I am. Whether I'm in an aircraft or answering silly questions or in a crowded city, if I want to be there, then the mind becomes still. At times I wonder, "Why do I have to do this? This is stupid stuff!" If I do that, of course I suffer. So instead I say, "No, I want to be here," and this gives rise to an incredible sense of peace and freedom. Therefore, when you're sitting in your room and the mind isn't still, don't make a problem out of it; simply say, "I want to be here," and then it does become still.

When you want to be right here, right now, you're developing freedom. You're practicing the third noble truth—you're ending craving and stopping the doer. It's a very powerful strategy: wherever you are and whatever you're doing, just ask yourself, "Do I want to be here or do I want to be somewhere else?" Every time the answer is that you want to be somewhere else, you're creating *dukkha*. That's simply the second noble truth of the Buddha. Every time you think, "I'm happy to be just here," you're ending some of the coarser manifestations of suffering. You're following the Buddha's teaching and the third noble truth.

When you're content in this moment, it's amazing what the here and now can teach you. My experience is that by just sitting down and wanting to be here, a *nimitta*—that beautiful old friend—comes up straight away, simply because the mind is still. You've understood that stillness is the same as the mind not moving, the same as not wanting anything and not trying to be somewhere else. Still, most people tend to think, "I'll get there; I'll do this and I'll do that, and then stillness will come later on." But it never comes later on. You can only build stillness now, and the only way to do that is by allowing this moment to be. Whatever the moment is like, you should say, "This is good enough; I want to be here in this moment, right now." It doesn't matter what you're experiencing; what matters is whether you want to be here or somewhere else.

So you can be completely free in a prison cell or you can be in prison in a five-star hotel. It's so nice to know that in any place, with any state of mind, you can always be free. Understand that and you understand how wisdom can free you. This is the *anālaya* of the third noble truth, having no place where anything can stick. This is the real meaning of detachment; this is enlightenment stuff.

Be Free of the Past

It's remarkable how we become prisoners of the past. For example, you might ask someone, "How are you doing?" and the answer is, "I'm feeling terrible." What does this mean? It usually means they've *had* a terrible day and they're carrying the past into the present. Please don't do that. Don't allow anything to stick, whether it happened a moment ago, five minutes ago, or hours ago. If you've had some wonderful meditations, don't allow those to stick either. If you think, "Wow, at last I did it; I'm really getting into it now," you're just creating the causes for failure in the future. Your job is to be free, not to carry around the so-called attainments or failures of the past. In Buddhism, as a meditator, you don't need to define yourself by success or failure; you can be completely free. Isn't it great to know that this is possible?

Develop this amazing ability to completely let go of everything—*anālaya*—so you don't stick to things. When you don't stick to anything, the "you" just fades away and disappears. What do you think of yourself? Who do you think you are? What are your qualities? How have you done so far in your meditation? These questions have no validity; they're judgments based on the assumption of an "I" and a "mine." When we believe such judgments and take them seriously, they only create suffering for us. You've done that far too many times. Don't give yourself a report card and then believe in it. Just be free.

Being free means you don't take your past seriously. What is the past anyway? It's only your memories, and your memories are just a way of looking at the past—you don't know exactly what happened. If you're in a good mood and you look at the past, you remember all the lovely things;

if you're in a bad mood, you remember all that went wrong. When you look at the past, perception is always selective—that's its nature—and you only pick up the things that resonate with your present mood. When someone first comes to a Buddhist monastery to ordain, he thinks, "This is such a beautiful place—why doesn't everyone come and stay here?" When other people disrobe he thinks, "How on earth can they disrobe? It's such a wonderful place. They must be crazy—out of their minds." Then the day comes when *he* disrobes, and now he thinks, "Why does anyone stay in this dump? This really sucks. This is an awful monastery, and people are so brainwashed. Can't they see it?" He's looking at the past—in this case, his accumulated memories of the monastery—with the mood of the present. You can't trust that, and what you can't trust, you can't take seriously.

In fact, what you don't take seriously isn't worth "taking" at all—let it go and you're free. Use your wisdom—your understanding of the nature of the past—to be absolutely, completely, 100 percent free. Then we're all on this wonderful level playing field: there are no great meditators or stupid meditators. In the present moment of meditation, I'm no different from anyone else. It's wonderful to be free and have no reputation—to have nothing to live up to, worry about, or feel guilty about, and nothing to fix up. You are completely free and empty. If you think and practice like this—carrying no burdens and being peaceful—meditation is so easy.

Sometimes people build up failure. Because they think they've failed in the past, they become people doomed to fail. I remember an experiment from my days as a schoolteacher where kids of equal intelligence were separated into two classes, class A and class B. The class A kids thought they had been put in the class for clever kids, because they had been told they had the better test results. The class B kids thought they were in the class for dummies, because they had been told their results were worse. Originally the children were at the same level academically, but after they were separated, the test results of the class A kids improved and the results of the class B kids deteriorated. Be careful of that psychology. Once you start thinking of yourself as a failure or thinking that you can't meditate, that becomes the reason why you can't meditate. Let it all go; abandon it. Be free of the past by reminding yourself that this moment is all you've got. Be happy to be just here, no matter what you're experiencing.

When you practice in this way, you discover that even the experience of pain is a result of your attitude and the way you look at things. The Buddha said that one should know *dukkha* completely. When you know the present moment completely, you can say, "Māra, I know you," and your pain vanishes. It's very hard to change a person, a situation, or a place, but you don't have to. What you can change is the way you look at things. You just need a new perspective, a moment of wisdom, and you see it all differently. The suffering fades and disappears, and meditation becomes easy.

When my meditation isn't getting anywhere, I sometimes ask myself, "What's going on, what's happening?" It sorts itself out straightaway, because as soon as wisdom recognizes the problem, it breaks up the blockages. The next moment is really peaceful, and you're off, getting into deep meditation. This is the power of true wisdom. If it really is insight, if it really is wisdom, it will give rise to *upasama*, a calm state. The problem is seen, and you can say, "Māra, I know you." Māra doesn't slink away—he just vanishes.

Give One Hundred Percent

These are some of the techniques we use to lead us to deeper meditation. Anyone can do it. Try using wisdom when you're having a terrible time or you can't get into deep meditation—you'll be surprised. Be happy to be here and be sharp enough to do it properly; don't mess around. Just say, "Okay, I'm going to give this a go; I'm going to be happy to be just here." Give it 100 percent—let go of the past, don't try to get anything, and have no expectations. Just allow things to disappear.

Give 100 percent and you'll find that it works. Not only do you get the quick payoff of peaceful meditation, but you also get more wisdom. It's not the Buddha's wisdom anymore, nor Ajahn Chah's wisdom, nor mine—it's your wisdom. You've done something and it's working. The mind is becoming clever, sharp, and wise, and it's recognizing the way to freedom.

The Buddha said that you should know the gratification and the danger in the five *khandhas* and the six sense bases, and that you should know the escape (SN 22:26–28; SN 35:13–18). The most important thing is the escape. You don't escape by using willpower, by being a strong, macho meditator who can sit through pain and force the mind through things. The way from ignorance and delusion to *nibbāna* is wisdom. Wisdom leads to peace and stillness, and the stillness reinforces the wisdom. Little by little, you get more mindful, peaceful, and blissful. The greater the mindfulness, the deeper you see. This beautiful path is so much fun and so interesting. Remember that you can do it; and you *will* do it, as long as you use your wisdom faculty. Don't keep banging your head against a brick wall—bricks are much harder than skin, bone, and gray matter. If you want bliss, peace, and freedom, use wisdom—it's far more powerful.

Pacification and the Insights that Follow 6

••• ————————————————————————————

Y OU CAN GRASP MUCH of the *Dhamma* by reading about it in books or studying the *suttas*. That's important, but it only gives you an external view. What you really need is to see for yourself how the mind works. You need to understand through direct experience where frustration, boredom, and restlessness—and also good qualities like stillness—come from. When you understand this process, you grow in insight. But to get there you have to develop calm and peaceful states of mind. The deeper that peace and stillness are, the more you understand the true nature of things.

Understanding Cause and Effect

For those who haven't yet experienced deep meditation, a useful simile to reflect on is that of the young person who takes apart a clock or radio to find out how it works. Once he has taken it apart and has it in bits, he has a rough idea of how it works. So if you're having problems in your meditation—going to pieces, as it were—don't worry, because this gives you a chance to find out how you work. And to find this out is to understand the cause-and-effect mechanism of the human body and mind.

But remember: you need peace and stillness to gain any real understanding. There's that old simile of the tadpole in the lake: if you were born in water and you've spent your entire life in water, you can't possibly know what water is like. It's only when the tadpole becomes a frog and comes out of the water that it can understand what water is. In the same way, it's only when things start to disappear in the deep states of meditation that you can understand what they are. It's the stillness of the mind, and the consequent disappearance of things, that give rise to great insight. Indeed, one of the synonyms for *nibbāna* is cessation—the calming of all *sankhāras*, the cessation of all things. *Sabbasankhārasamatha*—the calming of all *sankhāras*—is a wonderful concept to focus on. This is what *nibbāna* is—the *samatha*-ing, the calming, the tranquilizing, the settling, and the pacifying of all *sankhāras*. In this case, the term *sankhāra* refers to the effects produced by your actions of body, speech, and mind—that is, what you experience as a result of past *kamma*. But *sankhāra* can also refer to the whole process that causes the building up of *kamma*—that is, your willed actions of body, speech, and mind. Thus the word *sankhāra* has both an active and a passive sense.

Once you understand that your present situation has been created by causes, you can work that system of cause and effect in favor of peace, stillness, release, freedom, and enlightenment. To calm down those passive *sankhāras*, you must calm the active *sankhāras*—that process by which passive *sankhāras* are made. This means calming the will—the entire controlling and doing process—and using your wisdom to leave this moment alone and make peace with it. You open the door of your heart to this moment, no matter what it is—you're content, not demanding in nature, easily satisfied, and happy just to be here. It's not such a hard thing to do if you look at it rationally: the present moment is here anyway; since you can't really change it, you might as well accept it.

Pacify the Will and Reduce the Sense of Self

When you fight the present moment, you're doing the wrong thing—you're encouraging the will and making it stronger. A stronger will means a stronger ego and a stronger sense of self. But when the will is weakened, the ego is reduced, and when the will is eliminated, the ego is pacified and a major part of you just disappears. The vanishing of the sense of self is what we mean by *anattā*. This sense of self is both who you think you are in relation to others—the external ego—and, more importantly, the very essence of ego, or who you think you truly are inside. Ultimately, every peg you can hang the hat of a "me" or a "self" on is completely taken away. This is why the Buddha said that few people understand *sabba-saṅkhārasamatha*—it's scary for most people (MN 26.19).

To see your sense of self disappearing is a struggle in the early years of monastic life. It goes totally against the grain in a world where most people are actually seeking a clear and unique identity in their name, age, birthday, history, report cards, status, gender, and skills. You have worked hard to please others and to create a self that is acceptable in the world—acceptable to your friends, your peers, your parents, your teachers. You have a clear idea of who you are. You have the sense of being a solid entity, and now you're being told to disassemble it. It may seem as if you've just been wasting your time. Indeed, looking back at when I was at Cambridge, I now know that I was wasting my time trying to be somebody by studying to pass all those exams. You've probably been through that. And now that you're trying to disappear, that's the *kamma* you have to face.

But remember that you can't disappear through an act of will, saying, "I'm not going to be here anymore; this is going to be my last life." Since the will is what fashions the ego, it follows that even the will not to be—that is, the craving not to exist—actually perpetuates your sense of self. Like all will, that craving not to exist is a *saṅkhāra*, and all *saṅkhāras* create more things in the future. You'll never be able to end rebirth that way. The only way it can be done is by walking the path of meditation. By practicing and deepening your meditation, stage by stage, your sense of self, your ego, starts to vanish.

Meditation is so fundamental to the path of Buddhism that everything else, like *sīla* and even wisdom, can be regarded as a supporting factor. *Samādhi* is central because as you learn how to calm the mind down, you also learn little by little how to disappear, how to fade away. Of course, in the beginning it's hard to fade away—you want "to be" because that's been your sole purpose for innumerable lifetimes. That's why monastic life is set up for you to disappear; it helps you incline in that direction. You're just a monk in the middle of the line somewhere, or a novice at the end. You all wear the same clothes, and you all look alike. Even those people who come to the monastery regularly may not know your name. Do *you* know your name? Your name is the five *khandhas*, or the six sense bases; your name is impermanence, suffering, and nonself. If you understand that, then you understand that to move toward disappearance is to move in the right direction. And as you practice your meditation, you see that when even a little bit of you disappears, you have more peace, freedom, and joy. It's that joy and happiness—that sense of freedom and profound truth—that are the carrots that keep you moving deeper toward the pacification of all *saṅkhāras*. Even if you only pacify them a little bit, you can sense that you're on the right path.

Pacify Things and They Disappear

I was recently asked about the meaning of *saddhā*, or faith and confidence. What we mean by *saddhā* is this: faith in the ending of all *saṅkhāras*, faith in cessation, faith in *nibbāna*. It's not so much a faith in the triple gem— the Buddha, *Dhamma*, and *Sangha*—but rather a faith in what these are pointing to. Real faith is faith in cessation and in the end of suffering, and faith that these things can be achieved. If you have faith in the possibility of calming all *saṅkhāras*, then that possibility is real. How do you get that faith? It arises when you pacify the *saṅkhāras* a little bit, when you get into a deep and peaceful meditation. Eventually the *saṅkhāras* settle down to the point where they're simply not there anymore. When you fully pacify something, you calm it so completely that it disappears.

My own body is a good example. I'm getting older, so oftentimes when I sit down my body aches or my nose itches. But as I sit there, those feelings start to disappear. After a while the whole body is gone, and it's a profound relief. Years ago, there was a person on one of my retreats whose hands disappeared—she couldn't feel her hands! Well done! Little *saṅkhāras* were being calmed down. She put aside the fear and the shock and, when asked how it felt, she said it was beautiful and liberating.

When these kinds of happiness and peace come up, you gain faith in the path of calming things down and letting them go. As you follow that path, you learn how to calm yet more *saṅkhāras*. Why did this part or that part of the body disappear? It disappeared because you weren't getting involved in it or trying to change it or make it comfortable; you just ignored it completely, let it be, and disengaged from it. It's like trying to hold a glass of water still. No matter how hard you try, that water will never be absolutely still. It's only when you put the glass down—when you let go of the will—that the water becomes still all by itself. In meditation, when things get still, they disappear. You understand that when you pacify the active part of the *sankhāras*—the doing, the will, the choosing, the making—the resulting passive *sankhāras* vanish. The whole path becomes the art of gradual vanishing.

Pacifying Time

Time is a great torturer of human beings. How many days of the retreat are left? How much longer is this chapter? When can I go to the toilet? When can I go to sleep? How many hours do I sleep at night? How long until breakfast? How long until I can have a cup of tea? All this worrying about time just crucifies people. You need to calm time down.

It's the will or craving that creates the future, and it's ill will that creates the past. When you let go of the will, time starts to vanish, and it's a beautiful experience. You get the great insight of timelessness: you've been practicing meditation, but you have no idea for how long. You've been fully awake, but time had no meaning for you. You sit for two hours, three hours, or five minutes, and it's precisely the same. There's only one moment, and it's this one. That's all there is. Because you've pacified the active *sankhāras*—this business of willing—you've also pacified time. When time is pacified you meditate for two or three hours again and again without any problems. This can happen even if the meditation isn't very deep. And pacifying time is a profound experience with a great payoff: freedom, happiness, and bliss.

Pacifying Thought

Before you pacify time, you need to pacify the thinking and wandering mind. To do this you need a subtle type of will: the deliberate will not to do. It's the will to set up a guard at the gate of your mind, like a bouncer at a night club, saying, "There are these problems; don't let them come in." This sort of restraint is, at least initially, a type of willpower, a type of controlling. It's a conscious effort to subdue the mind, to curb its unwholesome tendencies. You just draw a line and put a guard there. You're like a gardener who, having planted many flowers and trees, guards and protects them to make sure nothing harms them. All you need to do is establish this guard with clear intention. Then, when the mind becomes still, the guard remains, protecting that stillness, valuing it, caring for it, and developing it. In this way, the moments of stillness, of peace without thinking, last longer and longer.

Something is lost when you stop thinking, and that something is "you." Many people measure themselves by their intelligence and their ability to think clearly and argue convincingly. But all they're really doing is pitting thinking patterns against each other, like two sumo wrestlers battling it out in the ring of concepts. True victory, however, comes from calming everything down. You still the mind to the point where concepts no longer arise. You have silence—you're peaceful and free.

Even if you can't pacify thinking for very long—even if it's only for a few seconds—please get to know how it feels. If you investigate it, you realize how nice it is. You begin to see that every time you have a thought, you're being harassed. It's like being married to a tyrant who's always tormenting you, or having a job where the boss is constantly haranguing you, telling you what to do, and even putting you down. It's so nice when all that is turned off. You delight in the quiet mind and grow in faith and confidence. Initially, you may be a bit frightened that you seem to disappear. Because thinking makes you feel like you're in control, not thinking may at first feel like taking your hands off the handlebars of a motorbike. You might wonder how you can keep your balance when thinking is not there to tell you what to do, to nudge you this way and that. But after a while, you see that it's okay not to think and control, that it's actually preferable to let go and disappear. In fact, it feels very good. In addition, you are getting your first insights into *anattā*, cessation, and fading away.

Pacifying Sensory Diversity

When you're ready to go further, the next step is to focus. Why do you have to watch the breath? Why can't you just stay in the silent present moment and leave it at that? Because of the diversity of the six senses and all their various objects, you are constantly bombarded by the noise of sensory experience. To calm that down, you first have to focus, turning from six senses to just two: the sense of touch (in the form of the breath) and the mind. Eventually you let go of the breath and reduce the focus to just the mind. This focusing of the mind is one of the great discoveries of the Buddha, because it's a crucial part of the way out of *saṃsāra*. The focused mind is another rung up the ladder of stillness.

The problem with nonverbal attention in its most undeveloped form is that the mind is still moving. This is because the mind is restless, seeking happiness now here, now there. The mind thinks that the next experience will be interesting or useful. It's this lack of contentment that drives people's lives, making them read books and watch movies, making them wander all over the world. What are they searching for? Look carefully and you'll see that wherever you go, things are essentially the same. The trees are the same and so are people. Why go to see the Great Wall of China? It's no big deal—walls are just walls. Or you take an expensive ride to the top of the Eiffel Tower. But a view is just a view. Why do people want to do these things? Often it's just something more to do—and wanting that next thing gives us a sense of who we are. We seek our identity in always going on to the next thing.

There's an old metaphor that describes life as a journey and meditation as the stopping of that journey. By stopping and sitting down somewhere and focusing on the breath, you can overcome the inclination of the mind to always want to go somewhere else. If you're really watching your breath, you can't feel any other part of your body. You don't know whether it's cold or hot, whether you've got an ache in your leg or a pain in your knee—you can't feel those things anymore. You're fully focused on the breath going in and out, unaware of anything else whatsoever. You've let go of diversity—you've pacified that movement of the mind that reaches out to the other senses. In other words, you've pacified four of the senses: seeing, hearing, smelling, and tasting. You've also pacified most of the sense of touch. All you have left is the breath, and now you're calming and pacifying that too.

You don't succeed in this process of pacification by controlling and holding on. I've tried that myself and it doesn't work. If you hold on to the breath, you can't sustain the meditation—you get tense and miss out on the joy of pacification. But if you practice properly, you're kind to the breath—you allow the process to happen all by itself. You pacify the causes of all these other things coming into your mind, until all that remains is the breath.

When you just watch the breath go in and out, something happens to your state of mind—it feels good; it feels peaceful. If you keep watching, joy arises. I call this the beautiful breath. It's beautiful, joyful, and happy because you're free from a whole heap of suffering. With this sort of experience comes a huge potential for insight, and you should mine that for all it's worth. Why is it that you can be so happy just watching the breath when most people have to watch football, read magazines, or go traveling to Paris and London? People worry about who is winning in the Olympic Games or the English Premier League. They worry about relationships, sex, and money, about needing to do this and that. All you have is the breath, and yet you're far happier than any of them. Why is that? It's because when you pacify things, you're letting go of the problems of life. All you have is the breath—and a beautiful one at that. There's nothing to do except be aware of it and allow it to calm down even further.

When you're free from burdens, happiness arises; when a whole heap of suffering ends, you feel a beautiful peace. As you calm the *saṅkhāras* down, little by little, you get more peace, more freedom, more happiness, and a greater sense of liberation. You realize, "Wow! This path of Buddhism is all about letting go, abandoning suffering, getting blissed out, and being free." You don't attach to the bliss but to the path of pacifying the *saṅkhāras*, because you know that this will lead you far, far deeper. You keep letting go of more *saṅkhāras*—the more the better. So far it's been fun; let's see how much more fun it can be. Take it from me, it gets to be enormous fun—more fun than you can imagine.

The Radiant Mind

As the breath calms down, you eventually let it go, and a beautiful *nimitta* appears. What is that *nimitta*? It's nothing other than the mind in a radiant state—what the *suttas* call the *pabhassara citta* (AN 1:49–52). It's the sixth sense released from the other five senses, like the moon released from behind the clouds. What do we mean by "released"? It means that the clouds aren't there anymore, that the five senses have been calmed to the point where they've disappeared, and all that remains is the mind. You can't feel the body—not even the breath. You haven't arrived here by controlling and worrying about the senses but by ignoring them and just watching the breath. You're simply focusing on the beautiful aspect of the breath, and this causes it to calm down. You're allowing the whole process to happen on its own. Then only the *citta*—the mind—remains.

The *nimitta* that arises in this state isn't just incredibly beautiful and blissful; it's also productive of important insights into the path of calming something until it disappears. Remember the simile of the tadpole: only now that the body and the five senses are fully pacified can you know what they truly are. Only now do you have a real understanding of what the Buddha taught. You also know why people sometimes think that the phrase *pabhassara citta*, the radiant mind, means "original mind," "the essence of all being," "God," or "cosmic consciousness" instead. It's because a *nimitta* is such an extraordinarily beautiful thing. But when you have the insight gained from experiencing a *nimitta* again and again and you know it fully, you'll realize it is a mistake to think of the radiant mind as a higher power or a transcendent reality. The radiance is simply the face of your mind when the five senses have been completely pacified.

The Jhānas: The Great Disappearing Act

All that's left at this stage is the mind, so the next step is to pacify the *citta* itself. Continue *samatha*-ing things and see how much more you can let go of. When you let go of the *nimitta*—not controlling it—you enter the *jhānas*, these amazing bliss states. A *jhāna* is the result of a very deep calming of everything—the body, the breath, the mind, and, most importantly, the will. The will cannot operate in *jhāna*; it has stopped. Because the will has stopped, you're not feeding it, so it starts to wither away. It's the same process as when you stop feeding people—they get smaller and weaker and eventually die.

If you practice *jhāna* consistently, you gradually progress from the first *jhāna* to the second and third and fourth, then on to the *āruppa* attainments, and eventually to *nirodha*. Since the will is no longer directing the mind, it starts to lose its momentum from the past, which is what stops you from getting deeper into *jhāna*. Just as when you cut off the fuel supply to your car, you go slower and slower until you eventually stop altogether, so too, as you progress through the *jhānas*, more and more things fade away. The *jhānas* are the great disappearing act of the mind. When you see this, it gives delusion a real kick in the pants. When you see the mind vanishing, you know that it too is a *saṅkhāra*—not created by a god or a self but by eons of doing and willing, lifetimes of action, speech, and mental activity. And now you're pacifying it, gradually allowing it to fade away. So getting into the *jhānas* and working toward *nirodha* until the mind ceases is what *sabbasaṅkhārasamatha* is all about. When you get there, nothing is left—no cosmic consciousness, no god, no experience, no perception, no feeling, no ultimate reality. Not even nothing remains. To understand this is to understand how *nibbāna* happens and why it is so extraordinarily blissful.

The great insights of the Buddha came from practicing *jhāna* and seeing things fade away. Getting into deep *samādhi* is, at least initially, the hardest part, because when you pacify the will, it seems as if you're disappearing. For this reason it's useful to practice skillful means like *anattā-saññā*, or nonself perception. It's very clear in the *suttas* that there's no such thing as a self; indeed, that's basic Buddhism. In scientific journals, too, psychologists tell you that there's no self; it's just a construct. So keep on plugging away at that understanding, and gradually you'll be able to let go of the will during meditation. The more you penetrate nonself, the easier it is to be still, and the more automatic is the process of pacification. It follows that an *arahant* gets into *jhāna* very easily and that even the *anāgāmī*, a nonreturner, does so without problems or difficulties.

Pacify All Saṅkhāras and End All Suffering

So little by little you pacify the mind, and at each step you reduce suffering. As long as there are *saṅkhāras* remaining, there will also be *dukkha*. As it says in the *suttas*, "All *saṅkhāras* are suffering" (e.g., AN 3:136). I don't know how you're feeling right now, but I know that it's *dukkha*. Even if you're inspired by what you're reading, it's still *dukkha*. Everything is suffering. If you can pacify everything then all suffering will disappear. As it all disappears and fades away, stage by stage, you get more of both faith and wisdom.

It's not that you start off with lots of faith and little wisdom and end up with heaps of wisdom but hardly any faith. Rather, the two grow together. As you get faith and confidence in this path, the insights accumulate, and as wisdom increases, that faith grows more and more. When you reach enlightenment, the confidence is utterly unshakeable.

But most people don't even have a little bit of faith, because most of them have too much "dust in their eyes," as the *suttas* metaphorically describe it (e.g., MN 26.21). This is especially true in our times when people are indulging and delighting excessively in worldly things. It's very hard for them to understand *sabbasaṅkhārasamatha*, the calming of the will and the calming of all things created by the will—that is, the calming of *saṃsāra*. It's hard for them to understand that aiming for this is worthwhile. But those who have calmed down enough, those who have only a little dust in their eyes, can see that this is the only path to happiness and freedom. Not embarking on this path means you experience endless busyness, tiredness, frustration, toil, and trouble—not just in one lifetime, but life after life after life, eon after eon. The Buddha said that the amount of tears you've cried is more than the waters in all the oceans of the world (SN 15:3). You've died so many times that if you piled up all your bones, the heap would be greater than a mountain (SN 15:10). The amount of blood you've shed from getting your head cut off is also more than the waters in the oceans (SN 15:13). That should give you a sense of *nibbidā*—repulsion or revulsion—toward this whole process of potentially endless suffering.

Fortunately, there's a way out. As you practice, you progress on that path little by little, and your confidence grows. Remember that it's all about pacifying things, calming things down. Establish a guard at each stage of meditation. Don't fool yourself into thinking that letting go means allowing fantasies to roll on or sleeping as much as you want. The non-doing is also a restraint, a protection, a guard, a bouncer. The best bouncers at nightclubs just need to stand there—they don't need to act, since their mere presence is enough to deter the riffraff. All you need to do is have mindfulness—strong, wise, protective, and caring—and the undesirable mind states will have no chance to arise. At the same time, little by little, your faith and wisdom will grow, and so will your sense of peace and freedom. You'll understand that this path and these deep meditations are the way to *nibbāna*.

There's no such thing as insight meditation devoid of *jhāna*. There's no such thing as another way, because there's only the eightfold path. There's only letting go, pacifying the *saṅkhāras*, and experiencing the results—the *jhānas*. As you experience the *jhānas* more and more, you eventually pacify every last *saṅkhāra*, and in the process you give up your false sense of self and your endless roaming around *saṃsāra*. You forsake all that suffering and aim for *nibbāna*. That's how insight comes from calming the mind. That's what we do, and that's what Buddhism is all about.

Appreciating the Bliss 7

. . .

"*SAMĀDHI* IS THE WAY; no *samādhi* is the wrong way" (AN 6:64). That's one of my favorite sayings from the *suttas*. It concerns the importance of the still mind. These days my preferred translation for *samādhi* is "stillness," because not only is stillness an accurate description of *samādhi*, but it's also evocative of what *samādhi* is really all about. That stillness carries with it a profound sense of happiness. You need to understand the nature of this happiness and improve your ability to recognize it.

Feel Your Way into Stillness

The opposite of stillness—*kummagga*, the wrong path—is agitation and restlessness, thinking, fantasizing, dreaming, and planning. The cause of that agitation is your doing things—your trying to control your body and mind. Even when you think you're not doing anything, you tend to follow your old bad habits. You don't even realize the doing is still going on. Because you're going with the current, you don't feel the flow. The only way you can really know that you've stopped the doing is by its effect: the mind is no longer agitated.

Much of the agitation we feel comes from our tendency to label and assess our experiences. In meditation you need to put aside this habit. Instead of thinking your way into meditation, you need to feel your way in—feel that the mind is getting more and more peaceful and more and more still. Don't name the experience as stillness. You know when the mind is acting because it's agitated and tense. But if the mind isn't acting, it slows down and becomes still, and then you know you're going in the right direction. If mindfulness is aware of that process, it's easy to feel your way into deeper meditation. As the stillness deepens, the mind changes to become beautiful, soft, and free. So the way into *samādhi* is to feel this whole process of calming the body and calming the mind, of relaxing and opening up.

Cooling Down the Senses

In the *Discourse on Burning* (SN 35:28), often known as the *Fire Sermon*, the Buddha declares that the five senses are on fire, along with the mind. They're on fire with craving, ill will, and the pain of existence. You can feel this fire moving and burning, the flames licking, harming people who touch it. When you meditate, you're putting out these flames by calming down the senses. And you're not only pacifying the five senses themselves but also the objects of the senses and the sense-consciousnesses—that is, every facet of the process of sensing.

When your meditation is working, you feel cool, soft, and peaceful. If you're restless, the body feels as if it's heating up, but when you become still in meditation, it feels like the temperature of the body goes down. It's similar with the aches and pains of the body. When you really calm down, when you get into *samādhi*, there are no aches and pains at all—the body is cool, calm, and still.

If the senses are on fire, what's the fuel? The fuel is your engagement with the senses, your involvement in them. The *suttas* talk about the hindrance of *kāmacchanda*. *Chanda* is what you do if you can't come to a *Sangha* meeting: you give your consent, your *chanda*, your approval for whatever is decided at the meeting. So *kāmacchanda* actually means you're approving of, agreeing to, and engaging in the five-sense process. When you get involved, caught up, and enmeshed in the five senses, the problems build up and you can never find stillness. But when you disengage—when you cut off the fuel and let go—the senses settle down.

If the meditation is working, after a while the body disappears. It's wonderful: you're sitting there and you can't feel your hands, legs, bottom, body, or head. You can feel neither aches and pains nor bodily pleasure; all of it has vanished. So when you disengage from your body, it cools down and becomes calm, and then it disappears.

Of course, this is frightening if you define yourself by your body, if you think you're strong, healthy, or fit. When you build up attachment to the body in this way, you keep holding on even when you get old and sick. You're stuck with this painful old body because you haven't developed the ability to let it go and allow it to disappear. So it's very useful to learn how to meditate when you're young. If you learn early on in life how to let the body go, it becomes much easier to do when you're old and sick. When you learn to let go to the point where the body disappears, you see that you are not the body. And that realization helps you let go in the future.

If you can't drop the body, ask yourself why. In the earlier chapter on dealing with distractions, I mentioned how Ajahn Chah used to say that it's not the sound that disturbs you; it's you who disturbs the sound. You get involved in it instead of just leaving it alone. It's the same with the aches and pains in the body and even with your thoughts: it's not that the thoughts disturb you, but that you disturb the thoughts by reacting to them. When you react, the process is perpetuated—your reaction is agitation, and agitation only creates more thinking. Engagement stirs up the mind. So disengage, stand back, and leave the mind alone. Remind yourself that whatever is happening is the result of old *kamma*—it has to happen; it's all cause and effect. There's no point in judging, measuring, or blaming yourself. If you can avoid this habit of getting involved, things settle down, the senses start to disappear, and you experience peace, freedom, and liberation.

Recognizing the Bliss of a Still Mind

The liberation you feel in meditation is wonderful—indeed, it's the highest pleasure you can possibly experience. But remember that the pleasure of meditation isn't of the same order as the normal pleasures of daily life—being deeper and more subtle, it has a different flavor. People sometimes miss out on the pleasure of meditation because they're looking for something familiar, something closer to their worldly experience. So during meditation, try to notice even tiny bits of pleasure, so that you get used to recognizing its special delights.

The Buddha compared worldly pleasure to the pleasure a dog gets from a bone smeared with blood (MN 54.15). It tastes like food but the nutritious, hunger-abating meat isn't there. The pleasures of the senses are like that: their taste promises satisfaction, but there's no substance. When your meditation starts to bite, you find the substance, the satisfaction. It doesn't just taste good, it's nutritious; it's not just a superficial and hollow flavor, it's the real thing.

You may have experienced that bliss before without fully appreciating it. It's a bit like those Magic Eye photos: initially they look two-dimensional, but when you learn to look at them in a different way, you see three dimensions instead. The three dimensions were always there, but you couldn't see them until you followed the instructions. In the same way, although you may experience still states of mind, it may take a while before you see how beautiful they are. Investigate the peace, and through repeated and continuous experience, you will start to recognize the sheer bliss of it. You appreciate the beginning of the end of suffering. The third noble truth is beginning to manifest for you in the calm, still mind.

Letting Go of the Desire for Bliss

One of the problems that arises when you start to experience the bliss of meditation is that you make the mistake of wanting it, of trying to make it happen. Once you've had an experience of stillness, you're seduced by the bliss and you want more. But this is just an old habit interrupting the path. So remember that the very desire for them stops you from getting into the deeper states of meditation. If you are not careful such desire will lead to lots of frustration. Remind yourself how you got into that peaceful state—not by wanting it, but by letting go of all wanting.

The first few times you get into these states, it seems to happen almost by accident—you don't expect it. It may not be your bedtime yet so you decide to sit for half an hour, since there is nothing else to do. Or maybe you're just killing time, so you sit down and do nothing. It might even be quite noisy around you. You can become peaceful in what seem to be the most weird or unlikely situations. After a while you realize why: it's not the noise or the discomfort that hinders your meditation; it's your attitude. It's because you are present in the moment—not expecting anything, not trying to get anywhere, the craving gone—that you become still and experience the beauty of that state.

The Buddha said that craving is the cause of suffering, and now you see it in practice. You understand craving directly as a movement of the mind. You see that the movement of the mind—the craving, the agitation, the involvement, the *upādāna*, or taking up of things—is fueling the process of suffering. Because you see this very clearly in your meditation, the movement of the mind just stops in its tracks. You're not taking anything up; you're not getting involved or attaching; you're not building up your sense of self or controlling; you're not taking notes or assessing your progress. That which asks "How am I doing?" or "What am I supposed to be doing next?" just calms down. When you see the source of those agitating assessments and you calm it down, you're off into deep meditation.

The more you follow this procedure of stilling the mind, the more bliss you experience, and meditation becomes truly fun. You start to taste some of the most delicious experiences available to anyone, and you begin to understand the immense value of periods of retreat or even monastic life. If you taste powerful bliss—like the bliss of a bright *nimitta*—that's worth years and years of your time, and it gives you a real sense of meaning. You may become a millionaire, fall in love, and have kids, yet you still wonder what the point is. Those things are not solid. They're just another bone smeared with blood: their taste promises so much but they never deliver. Deep meditation is different. Even if you get into *jhāna* just once, it satisfies you for years. It may sound strange, but when you know what I'm talking about, it makes perfect sense. Deep meditation is powerful and fulfilling—you've touched something amazing.

The Bliss of Things Disappearing

It's possible that some Hindu and Christian mystics have gotten into *jhāna*. At the very least, they have had some deep meditation experiences. The experience is so powerful for them that they call it union with God. It's not union with God, so why do they say that? They say it because the experience—the mind totally unified, the feeling of bliss and power, the absence of an "I"—is incredibly profound. Such extraordinary experiences are the result of non-doing, of being completely relaxed. You've let things calm down to the point where they fade away and disappear. Thinking is impossible and hearing has ceased. At the time, you don't even know that this is the case, since such knowledge requires movement of the mind. Only when you recall the event afterward can you reflect on what actually happened.

The Buddha said, "Patience is the highest austerity" (Dhp. 184). "Patience" here doesn't mean enduring pain or fasting because you think torturing yourself must be good. That's not what the Buddha meant. What he meant by "patience" is the simple act of watching without getting involved in any way. The sign of real patience is that things vanish and you become still. When stillness arises, your ego starts to fade. To be somebody, you have to do things; but when you stop doing things—when you're fully patient—you vanish. You're no longer defined by your past nor imprisoned by your hopes and plans for the future. When you stay in the present moment and do nothing, you're free—disappearing, vanishing, merging in emptiness. You understand that the end of suffering cannot possibly entail more things: it can only be nothingness, emptiness, disappearance. While you're reading this, if you're really getting into it, your mind is empty of your room, your duties, your family—everything apart from the reading. Even with this sort of emptiness, you're getting a small taste of freedom.

There is a story of a monk who sat under a tree, saying over and over, "Oh what bliss, oh what bliss" (Ud. 2:10). Because that monk was a former king, some monks passing by thought he was recalling the happiness of kingship. In fact, it was the other way around: he was reflecting on the absence of royal duties and fears and thinking about how wonderful it was *not* to be king. When you focus on what has been left behind, you feel a sense of freedom and happiness. The happiness of fading away and disappearance shows you the value of emptiness. You notice what is no longer there and the freedom this brings. This is the Buddha's own description of emptiness meditation (MN 121).

Think of how good you feel at the end of an illness when you're released from the hospital. Many years ago, when I was still a young monk living in Thailand, I had scrub typhus. I was in the hospital for a month feeling miserable. When I was released, I was still physically weak, but it felt so nice. It was a happiness born of something disappearing: the suffering of typhus was gone. For once, I actually appreciated my health. When you're in constant good health, you tend not to appreciate it unless you consciously reflect on the absence of pain or illness. In the same way, the monk who was an ex-king only recognized the bliss of freedom when he recollected the fears and burdens of kingship.

Try to apply this perspective in your meditation. When you're sitting with your eyes closed, recognize the freedom of not having to worry about your family, your body, your duties, or anything other than just being here. You're free: it's a holiday, a holy moment. Get off on that pleasure. When the fantasies stop and the thinking pauses, get off on that. When you do, you're appreciating the pleasure of things disappearing. You understand what we mean by *nirāmisa sukha*, the happiness of letting go, the pleasure of things disappearing.

The Bliss of Renunciation

In the *Araṇavibhaṅga Sutta* (MN 139.9), the Buddha distinguishes between two types of pleasure: sensory pleasure—the pleasure of getting things, of getting involved in things—and the pleasure of *Dhamma*—the pleasure of renunciation, of things disappearing and fading away. I had one of my first experiences of the pleasure of *Dhamma* very early on in life, when I was still at school. We had half-day holidays: if you'd been a good boy, you got the afternoon off. On those days I would do all my homework during the lunch break to get it out of the way. Then, with all my duties completed, I had nothing to do in the whole world. That freedom from all responsibility made those half-day holidays the most memorable afternoons of my early life. What I was experiencing as a thirteen-year-old boy was the pleasure and happiness of things disappearing.

Practice meditation like that. Don't think of what you need to do next and all the deep stages of meditation you have yet to reach. If you do that, you don't appreciate the present moment, and the path to the deeper states is closed off. Don't burden yourself, especially when you're on retreat, thinking that you have to get *jhāna* or that you have to become enlightened. Instead of putting pressure on yourself, just be at peace: no more goals or demands; nothing in the world to do except to watch one breath and appreciate it. You're simplifying your state of mind to the maximum. When you do that, you're clearing the way into *jhāna* and out of *saṃsāra*.

Appreciating simplicity is like planting a seed: things start to develop by themselves. As you keep simplifying your state of mind, it becomes more and more pleasant. The meditative happiness, which at first you couldn't see clearly, now enchants and captures the mind. That's what it's supposed to do. Don't worry about getting attached to it—as the *suttas* say, this happiness is beneficial and necessary, not dangerous (MN 66.21). It has a quality of liberation—when you cut away at craving, the ego can't survive, and you're led deeper and deeper into letting go and detachment. This is a happiness that feels naturally pure, leads to stillness, and inclines toward freedom.

The Bliss of Cessation

As you go deeper on this path of things fading away, you understand the brilliance of the Buddha's teaching. When you recognize that the six senses, including the mind, are like fire, you naturally respond by cooling them down until there's no fire left, no fuel, nothing. The more the senses disappear, the more freedom you feel, and as part of this process, the *jhānas* just happen. You understand that this path is a movement toward emptiness. You realize that "nothing is worth holding on to" (SN 35:80). Even to understand this is beautiful, but far more beautiful is to experience it.

Sometimes you think you can't possibly become more still, but then you do anyway. Fewer things are moving and more things are vanishing; the mind becomes ever more still. Superlatives can't keep up with the deeper experiences of meditation. The mind gets more and more empty, more and more still, more and more blissful. You understand why *nibbāna*—the cessation of all things—is the ultimate bliss and happiness. The path of calm and insight is the happy path—the happiest path you can possibly tread—and as you go deeper it only gets happier. When people get onto it and the practice takes off, it has a snowball effect: rolling downhill, the snowball gets bigger and faster; the practice goes deeper and deeper. Getting started is the only difficult part.

Once you start appreciating the bliss, you begin to experience all the *Dhamma* in the world right there in your own heart. You see the whole *Tipiṭaka* unfolding as the senses disappear and the mind enters the bliss states. The *khandhas* are seen for what they are. You understand why the senses are on fire, why they are suffering, and you get fed up with it all. You get a sense of repulsion, *nibbidā*; from *nibbidā* you get *virāga*—the fading away—and from *virāga* you get cessation—things ending. This is how you become free. The path—insight, bliss, deep meditation—is right there in your heart. All you need to do is follow the instructions: Sit down, shut up, watch, and don't get involved. Gradually, the meditation experience will open up all by itself.

Recognizing True Wisdom 8

◆ ◆ ◆

IT'S IMPORTANT TO UNDERSTAND what *paññā*—wisdom—is, and how to recognize it. True wisdom is powerful because it tells us about the practice of meditation and the Buddhist path in general. The function of wisdom can be appreciated by considering the triple practice of *sīla*, *samādhi*, and *paññā*—virtue, stillness, and wisdom—from two different perspectives. The practice can be seen as sequential: you first perfect virtue, then *samādhi*, then wisdom. Alternatively, they can be regarded as factors that support each other: the practice of virtue gives power to *samādhi* and wisdom; success in *samādhi* strengthens virtue and wisdom; and as wisdom grows, it provides ever-increasing support to virtue and *samādhi*. The further along the path you go, the more the three factors support each other. This is because wisdom has the power to create stability in the other two factors. So this chapter is about how wisdom—when it really is true wisdom—makes the practice of virtue easier and creates greater stillness in the mind.

The Effects of Wisdom

One of my favorite teachings from the *suttas* is the Buddha's answer to the question "What is *Dhamma*?" His response was simple but profound: "It is whatever leads to complete repulsion, fading away, cessation, peace, higher knowledge, enlightenment, and *nibbāna*" (AN 7:83). On that list you find peace, *upasama*. Peace is the beautiful tranquility in which you just flow through the day with no disturbances or problems. Whatever you do—whether you're meditating, sleeping, or eating, whether in company or in solitude—there's a sense of evenness, an absence of problems and difficulties. *Sama,* the last part of *upasama,* means "even," as in an even path, a path without bumps. This points to an excellent definition of wisdom: it is the understanding that leads to an even, peaceful, and balanced life.

A long time ago, when I was still a layperson, I used to visit monks who could spout incredibly inspiring teachings. But when I looked at them, I could see that they weren't peaceful. So much for their wisdom! Although they were inspiring and made good sense, the Buddha's standard is that a person's wisdom should be judged by the effect it has on his or her life. If that wisdom doesn't have the effect of settling the problems and difficulties in one's life—of creating a sense of ease, well-being, space, happiness, peace, and freedom—then it cannot be the real thing. In the *suttas,* too, you find that monks and other ascetics who were "haggard, lean, with a bad color, with the veins all standing out" were either ill or not practicing properly, whereas the monks who had wisdom—who were practicing properly—were "smiling and cheerful, sincerely joyful, plainly delighting, their faculties fresh, living at ease" (MN 89.12). So from a Buddhist point of view, wisdom by definition must lead to a general sense of ease.

Wisdom also leads to virtuous behavior. In my early years in Thailand, when Buddhism was still considered highly alternative among Westerners, some very radical people joined our monastery. Some of them argued against many of the monastery's rules and regulations, saying that they just led to repression and had nothing to do with wisdom. But after many years of practice, especially if your meditation and the accompanying insights are deep, you see that those rules and regulations are just an expression of how peaceful coexistence comes about in a community.

The point I wish to make is that you know people's wisdom by their ability to be at peace, not by the content of their speech. The whole path of Buddhism leads to the calming of the mind, to being at peace with the body, to being free in this world. This is the state of a wise person. If you have true wisdom, you're peaceful and happy: you have solved the problems of life.

Cause and Effect

Through meditation and stillness, you acquire the deep data from which you derive insight into cause-and-effect relationships. Much of the Buddha's teaching is about understanding cause and effect, or where things come from and why they arise. As disciples of the Buddha, if there's a problem, we investigate it. We use our reason and experience to find out where the problem came from and where it leads. If we see that it leads to a negative or harmful state of body and mind, then we know that it is unwholesome and not connected with wisdom. Next, we investigate backward, to see the process by which that problem arose.

When you have enough mindfulness, peace, and wisdom, you see a whole series of causes and effects. You understand where anger, guilt, depression, and fear come from; you see how they grow inside of you. When you see these things clearly, you're able to catch them early; and because you know they are unwholesome and unskillful, you're able to do something about them.

Once a negative mental state has taken hold of your mind, you can't do much except stand back and allow it to pass. The most important thing is to make sure you're aware of it so that you can lessen the problem the next time it arises. This was the practice of one of my fellow monks in Thailand. He had a very difficult time in his first few years, but I admired him because he stood up to the defilements in his mind. Even though sometimes he had so much suffering that he thought he was going to go crazy and that he would have to leave, he stayed. The first time he was going through a really difficult period, he expected the problem to get worse and worse, but to his surprise and relief, it just petered out. It ended because he hadn't fed into it. He now had a direct experience of the impermanent nature of those states.

Importantly, he also realized that the dark state hadn't gone away forever. He understood it as a process: he saw how it arose and what kept it going. He saw that he didn't need to do anything to stop it; he just needed to avoid feeding the fire and allow it to burn out on its own. Because he developed this insight, the next time he had a dark state of mind, it was much easier to deal with. He remembered his previous experience and realized that this problem, too, would end by itself. He didn't make it more than it was, wasn't afraid of it, and didn't get upset by it. Consequently, he found it easier to endure, and because of his greater insight, the problem wasn't as intense and didn't last as long as before. And when it passed away again, his wisdom was further reinforced. Each time the problem arose, it was shorter and easier to bear, until eventually the problem disappeared altogether. That's a beautiful example of wisdom in practice—simple wisdom, but wisdom nonetheless. Every time we're able to reduce or overcome our problems, that's wisdom at work.

Recognizing and Avoiding the Snakes

We should use our understanding of these negative states of mind to inform our mindfulness. When we're mindful, we see these mental and physical states growing, and because of our understanding, we can take remedial action before they get too entrenched. Another monk from my early years in Thailand had been a soldier in the Vietnam War. He was shot in the back of the head, lost a portion of his brain, and became epileptic. As a monk, he used his mindfulness to see the signs of an epileptic fit earlier and earlier. The earlier he caught the signs, the more opportunity he had to take another path—to rest, go to his room, or whatever it was that he came up with—so they wouldn't lead to a fit. Over time he had fewer and fewer fits. Eventually, he got to the point where he caught them so early that they stopped altogether. He had used his mindfulness to generate the wisdom that solved the problem. And that's the point I'm trying to make: you can use your mindfulness and wisdom together to avoid the problems before they get to you.

During my early years in Thailand, there were lots of snakes in Wat Pah Pong. We often didn't have sandals because they fell apart so quickly, even though we did our best to tie them together with pieces of string or old strips of cotton cloth. At times we didn't even have flashlights—we would use them until they were really dead and couldn't generate even a flicker of light. Then we had to walk barefoot on those snake-infested paths with only the starlight to help us find our way. But because I knew there might be snakes on those paths, I set up my mindfulness to look out for them and regard them as dangers to be avoided. Because of that, I never got bitten. I had informed my mindfulness and used a basic form of wisdom to make sure that if I saw any snakes I would make a detour.

You can do exactly the same thing to avoid being bitten by negative states of mind: you use mindfulness to stay aware of the dangers. You know that negative mental states will not lead to peace but to more disturbances; they are bad habits that destroy happiness and lead to suffering. And like snakes, once they get you, you're in big trouble. So use your mindfulness to recognize these negative states as soon as they arise and then take another route—that is, use a strategy to avoid them. In this way you reduce your problems. Your wisdom is creating a more peaceful, happy, and healthy life, and you flow through the world with ease.

Although a happy and healthy life is its own reward, there are further, more profound benefits from overcoming negative mental states. Because negative states are suffering, people often react to them with further negativity, leading to feelings of anger, depression, or guilt. If you didn't experience those negative states—that suffering—to begin with, you wouldn't feel the guilt. When you use mindfulness and wisdom to reduce or even resolve that suffering, you don't need to escape into fantasies or daydreams, and it's easier to keep the precepts and retain a pure mind. This in turn makes you more joyful, and it becomes easier to get into stillness and strengthen your wisdom. You achieve a self-supporting cycle that gets more and more powerful as you go along. And it's all because you're using your wisdom.

The Fault-Finding Mind

Watch out for negativity, because it feeds the fault-finding mind. Fault-finding is an attitude that arises and then gets hold of you, just as a snake might, and it poisons your mind. Once the fault-finding is well established, there's no end to the things you can find fault with. In the *suttas* you find that people found fault even with the Buddha! You may have the most perfect of monasteries, the most hard-working of teachers, the best food in the world, and the most comfortable hut, yet you can still find fault with all of it. As a young monk I would sometimes find fault even with Ajahn Chah, and afterward I would feel really stupid. If I could find fault with him, the wisest and most selfless person I had ever met, then it was quite clear that the problem was with me, not with Ajahn Chah.

Once you get into fault-finding, you also end up applying it to yourself. On retreats, people often find fault with their practice: "I still haven't achieved anything; I've just been sleeping for the last few days." Be careful, because fault-finding soon leads to guilt. Guilt in turn leads to punishment, and then your practice stalls—at best.

But when we follow the Buddhist teachings, we use the AFL code: Acknowledge, Forgive, and Learn. If we make a mistake, instead of beating ourselves up, we simply acknowledge it: "All right, I was late. I slept in this morning." Next we really forgive. There's no point to punishment—wisdom, real wisdom, knows that punishment just makes the problem worse by creating more unskillful states of mind. When we forgive, we're letting go, and that leads to peace. Only if something leads to peace, freedom, and release is it a wise thing to do. When you see that fault-finding is leading you in the wrong direction, you learn to avoid it altogether in the future.

I recently read a book about various therapies developed around the idea of finding the source of your present problems in past lives. The problem with that sort of approach is that it's often endless. It's much more productive to simply let go of the past or, even better, to recall that part of the past that was pleasant. You learn far more from your pleasant memories of past success and happiness than you ever learn from your suffering. When you remember what worked in the past, it encourages you, stops the fault-finding, and illuminates the causes of success. So drop all the lazy and restless meditations, and remember and learn from the good ones. Even if you only had one good meditation and you only watched the breath for five minutes, remember that! It encourages, informs, and leads you to greater peace. It's the way of wisdom.

So we should see the fault-finding mind as a problem, a snake, a danger to be avoided. It's common in the West to think that fault-finding is good. People sometimes write books with a fault-finding attitude in order to destroy authority, tradition, and institutions. Some years ago, someone visited Wat Pah Nanachat for three or four weeks and then wrote a book about his experiences. He really blasted the monastery and Ajahn Chah. He focused on everything that he thought was wrong, and consequently the book was completely unfair and unbalanced. People do this sort of thing because there's a certain pleasure in fault-finding. But be careful, because the danger far outweighs the pleasure. When you know this, you realize the fault-finding mind is a snake, and you can start to avoid it in the future.

In my experience, as much as 90 percent of monastic life—and by extension, any real practice of Buddhism—is about understanding the fault-finding mind. This includes understanding where it comes from, how to avoid it, and how to develop the positive mind—how to see the nine hundred and ninety-eight good bricks, not just the two bad ones, in a wall you've constructed. Instead of fault-finding, try to understand human beings, yourself included, and have forgiveness and loving kindness. See yourself as just a person on the path, this poor little being who has suffered a lot already and who doesn't want more suffering. If you can be at peace with your suffering, you'll find that the fault-finding decreases.

My own ability in meditation comes from my attitude of saying, "This is good enough," to whatever I'm experiencing. Ability in meditation is all about attitude: as long as I can watch the breath, that's good enough for me, and the *jhānas* are just a bonus. So when you meditate, be contented and easily satisfied. This is not being lazy, but simply following the instructions in the *Mettā Sutta* that I mentioned in chapter 4. You're developing the causes that undermine the fault-finding mind. When you undermine the fault-finding mind, the two major defilements of anger and guilt are weakened considerably, and you experience a corresponding sense of freedom.

Right Thought, Right Intention

Since you have a mind, you also inevitably have thoughts. As Ajahn Sumedho pointed out years ago, right thought doesn't mean having no thoughts—except in deep meditation—but rather having thoughts of renunciation, kindness, and gentleness toward all beings, including your-self. Even the Buddha had such thoughts. When your heart feels free, it's because you've practiced these three kinds of right thought. And because these thoughts lead to peace and stillness, you know they have arisen from wisdom.

Wisdom can always be measured by the qualities of mind it produces, and those good qualities in turn produce more wisdom. Whatever wisdom I have as a teacher has arisen from a still mind. Stillness gives you profound data to work with and the ability to think clearly. It increases your understanding of the path to the rejection of the sensual world, to the abandoning of things, to *nibbidā*, to tranquility, to *upasama*, to peace and freedom. You understand that this is the *Dhamma*, that this is the instruction of the Buddha.

When you meditate, please remember what wisdom is. The Buddha's teachings are there to keep you in line, to make sure you understand what wisdom is and what it's not. If something leads to well-being, tranquility, happiness, peace, and freedom, it must be a wisdom practice. But if negative qualities are created, then you're on the wrong track, and you're not practicing wisely. So investigate—find out what the wrong track is, and don't go there again; see it as a snake and avoid it. If you're on the wrong track right now, just be patient and still; you won't stay there for long. Instead of trying to discipline your mind with ill will, fault-finding, guilt, punishment, and fear, use something far more powerful: the beautiful kindness, gentleness, and forgiveness of making peace with life—in short, the *Dhamma* of the Buddha. The longer you live and practice like this, the more pure your heart will become.

This is the path. It's not that hard to follow. You've got the brains—use them. You've got some mindfulness—strengthen it. You've got a natural kindness inside of you—develop it further. You have everything it takes to walk this path. Eventually great wisdom and a deep understanding will arise. When deep understanding arises, it's as if you've gone to a high altitude: you see more and you gain greater perspective than you ever had before. You're beginning to understand what the Buddha taught.

Happiness Comes from Disappearing 9

∴ ∴

WHILE THE BUDDHA gave his first teaching, the *Dhamma-cakkappavattana Sutta* (SN 56:11), Aññā Koṇḍañña became a stream-winner. A major focus of this *sutta* is explaining the scope of suffering, which the Buddha said "should be fully understood." Among the group of five monks who listened to that teaching, only Aññā Koṇḍañña understood fully and completely. Knowing suffering fully is difficult—we have a natural resistance to seeing this reality. Because of this, I think it's easier to become a stream-winner by focusing on nonself and the source of who we think we are.

Everything Is Conditioned

In the *Sammādiṭṭhi Sutta* (MN 9), the great monk Sāriputta hammers home the teaching of nonself. Using the framework of the four noble truths, he goes through every possible aspect of the mind and body, shows how each one of them is entirely dependent on a cause, and explains how that cause can be abandoned. This profound conditionality means that everything has a cause: there's no permanent self or god, nor anything else that is permanent. When you see that all things have a cause—a fuel and a base from which they grow—you also see that once that cause is eliminated, the thing itself disappears.

In the same *sutta*, Sāriputta goes through dependent origination and shows how even consciousness has a cause, and that without that cause, there would be no consciousness. This is a powerful statement because practically all people—that is, everyone apart from the *ariyas*—take consciousness, the knower, as their self. And because they identify with the knower, they cherish it and won't let it go.

The Nonself of the Five Senses

You can see your inability to let go when you're meditating. Why is it that you can't ignore an itch or an aching knee? Why can't you let go of sounds? Why can't you let go of the past and the future? Why can't you stop the restless mind? Instead of just trying to be still, understand why you're not. What is the cause of the restlessness, and where does it come from? Remember that this is the Buddhist path, a path of investigation. You won't be able to let go by using willpower; only by understanding things and tracing them back to their source can you let them go. What generates restlessness? Of course there are many sorts of causes, but if you keep investigating, you'll see that in the end it all comes down to the sense of a "you," the sense of an abiding self.

We can't let go because we're holding on to our body and mind: we think we own them. We are no more willing to let them go than people are willing to let a thief take their wallet. Think of how easy it is to let go of something that doesn't belong to you. If something has nothing to do with you and it goes, then that's all there is to it—it goes. So if you don't own consciousness, if you don't think consciousness is your most important possession, then you don't get concerned when consciousness starts to fade away during meditation. If sound-consciousness fades away and you don't hear anything, you have no inclination to alert the mind to turn on the sense of hearing. You're just not interested; you've let it go. When parts of the body fade away and you can't feel them, you're not concerned. You don't turn on the sense of touch, because you're quite willing to be without it.

Initially, this means going out of your comfort zone, because your normal way of experiencing the world through the senses is no longer available to you. But you're willing to go there because you have faith and because you are beginning to understand that the senses don't belong to you. The more you understand that the sense-consciousnesses are not you, the less you worry about them. If, however, we still think we own these things, we use them to build our sense of identity. We think we exist through activities like seeing and eating: sensory experience gives us a sense of being. It takes faith, and a little bit of trial and error, to abandon that outer layer of being consisting of the five sense-consciousnesses. When the sense-consciousnesses start to fade, our whole perception of being changes: we no longer live in the world. By living in the world I don't mean wheeling and dealing in stocks and shares, building a house, having sex, or watching movies. What I'm talking about is living in the world of the five senses: seeing, feeling, worrying about what people say, or being concerned about any other sensory object.

I stress this point because if you can see that you're not the sense-consciousnesses, that they have nothing to do with you, then it also becomes clear that they're not under your control. Too many people spend their whole lives trying to ensure that they don't see ugly things, hear unkind or harsh speech, or have painful experiences. They'll go to doctors and dentists, take aspirin or morphine, or do almost anything to avoid bodily pain—but they're never successful. They can't do it because these unpleasant experiences have causes like nature and *kamma*. The cause of old age, sickness, and death is birth. You have been born, so you're stuck: you're going to experience pain and old age, get sick, grow weak, and die. Since you can't escape these things, you need to accept them and give up the struggle.

When you understand that the senses have nothing to do with you, you naturally give up your concern for them and allow them to disappear—even the aches and pains. How can you be in great pain and still smile? If the senses have nothing to do with you, neither does the pain. And if the pain has nothing to do with you, it's not important to you, and you can simply ignore it. You only pay attention to something if you think it's important.

It's fascinating to consider what's important to people. When they're watching football or a movie on TV, they eat these TV dinners, but they don't even taste the food. It's just not important to them; the match or the movie is what's important. They might not even know what they're eating. Can you watch the breath with such focus while you're eating that you have no idea what you're eating? Can you contemplate the three characteristics of impermanence, suffering, and nonself to such an extent that you don't even notice the flavor of the food? The reason you notice the flavor is because you think it's important. And the reason it's important to you is that your sensory experiences build a sense of self, a sense of identity, a sense of being. But in your practice of Buddhism you're going in the opposite direction. When you contemplate and understand the teachings of the *Sammādiṭṭhi Sutta* (MN 9) or the *Anattalakkhaṇa Sutta* (SN 22:59), you see things in a different way. The five senses have nothing to do with you—they're turned on because of causes, which means they can also be turned off when those causes are eliminated. When they do turn off, it's no big deal—you're not concerned. You don't turn them on again; you let them go.

When the five senses disappear for a long period of time, you have entered *jhāna*. The Pali formula for the first *jhāna* includes the phrase *vivicc'eva kāmehi*—aloof, separated, distant, and disengaged from the activity of the five senses. You can't feel the body because the mind is beyond the reach of the five senses for the duration of that *jhāna* attainment. You see that the five senses aren't you, which is an important insight that begins to confirm the Buddha's teaching of nonself. If you haven't experienced a *jhāna* yet, if you can't let go to that point, ask yourself why. What's the cause of the attachment? What's the cause of your concern with the physical body, with sounds, feelings, fantasies, dreams, and inner dialogue? Remind yourself that this is all within the five-sense realm, and thus has nothing to do with you. Sense-consciousness continues because of causes, and one of its major causes is your interest and involvement in it—in other words, attachment. So cut it off and let it go.

Please keep in mind that attachment is like a rope: at one end is what you're attaching to, but at the other is where that attachment is coming from. Too often when we talk about attachment, we say we're attached to food, sex, movies, or sleeping, but we forget what's actually attaching to those things. What's on this end of the rope? It's your identification with things. The problem is the "I" inside: I need to sleep, I need to read books,

I need to listen to the radio—*I need.* If your meditation isn't deep, it's because the "I" is holding on to the sense-consciousnesses.

Success in meditation isn't just a matter of watching the breath hour after hour, finding a quiet place in the forest, controlling the temperature of your room, or sleeping just the right amount. The physical conditions may be perfect, but that's not enough—something else is needed. That something else is to see deeply that the five sense-consciousnesses have nothing to do with you. When you see that they're not your business, you stop playing with them, and then you abandon them and watch them fade away. When they fade away, you gain an important insight: the bliss of *jhāna* arises because a whole heap of suffering—the five senses—has disappeared.

Letting Go of Mind-Consciousness

The next step—and this is important, since many people get stuck at this stage—is to see the mind, the *citta*, exactly for what it is. Just as with other types of consciousness, the cause of the sixth type—mind-consciousness— is *nāmarūpa.* This is what Sāriputta described in the simile of the two sheaves of reeds leaning against each other (SN 12:67). *Nāmarūpa* is basically the object of consciousness, for consciousness is aware of feelings, perceptions, and the will; these are universal aspects of experience. *Nāmarūpa* and consciousness lean on each other: if you take one away, you remove the support of the other, so it vanishes too. Consciousness cannot be present all by itself, unaware of anything. If *nāmarūpa* disappears, so does consciousness. This is what you start to see when you enter the deeper *jhānas*: parts of the mind-consciousness vanish. When you see this, you won't get stuck in first *jhāna* because you know that even mind-consciousness has nothing to do with you.

Sāriputta said in the *Sammādiṭṭhi Sutta* that consciousness is of six types, that it has a cause, and that it does cease (MN 9.58). He also said that the way to the cessation of consciousness is the eightfold path. So the end of suffering includes the end of consciousness. By pointing this out, Sāriputta is really laying on the line what the *Dhamma* is all about.

It's one thing to lose the sensation in your hands, like that woman on my retreat did many years ago; but losing your consciousness—that really cuts all the way to the bone. But as the Buddha said, this is part and parcel of the end of suffering. It makes us sit up and take notice of the profundity of his teachings.

And it's not just consciousness that ends, but feeling and all the other factors of dependent origination, too. The Buddha said that if you practice the eightfold path, it leads to the end of all feeling, all pain, pleasure, and even neutral feeling or equanimity. It's very clear that the goal of Buddhism is not to achieve some state of bliss or equanimity for evermore, but full *parinibbāna*. You may think this is a bit too much, but the point is that you aren't losing anything; there isn't any "you" there in the first place. That whole illusion of "you"—you owning those feelings, you doing something, you as the center of this being—is now understood as just a cause-and-effect process. You're experiencing with the clearest possible mind state that there's no one in here whatsoever, and you bliss out on the way to *nibbāna*.

Suffering Is the Problem

Most people think that ending consciousness is a kind of spiritual suicide. But the point is that if you don't do it, you suffer like hell. You've got a choice: you can keep on suffering, or you can attain *parinibbāna*. When you understand the four noble truths and the suffering inherent in existence, you see that *parinibbāna* is really the only option.

When suffering manifests, craving is generated. Suffering is a problem that you feel compelled to do something about, that makes you move: from this place to that place, from being a layperson to being a monk, from being a monk to being a layperson. Suffering is what makes the world go around—if you weren't suffering, if you were completely content, you wouldn't need to move. That's why the more content and happy you are, the more still you are. The reason the *jhānas* are such incredibly still states is that they're so blissful there's no need to move, no need to seek happiness elsewhere. The degree to which you move physically or mentally is a sign of how much suffering you're experiencing. The more suffering you have in your meditation, the more restless you are. If there's no suffering or very little, you can sit for hours, peaceful and still. Why? Because when there's no problem, there's nothing to do.

So suffering is the thing that keeps you going from place to place, from birth to birth, trying to find a solution. Trying to find a solution to suffering is the meaning of life, but the end of suffering cannot be found in the world or in *saṃsāra*. There's no heaven realm where you can live happily ever after; and if you think about it, you'll realize that such a heaven realm intrinsically cannot exist. Take the most delicious food, or even the best of sex: if you indulge in it all the time, after a while you get bored. It's just the same thing again and again. You can't have only pleasure all the time, because any pleasure, any happiness, is dependent on what came before it. If you look deeply at what pleasure is, you'll see that it's just the pause between two occasions of suffering. The reason you enjoy your food is because you haven't eaten for a while and you won't be eating afterward. If you were continuously stuffing yourself twenty-four hours a day, would you even taste the food, let alone enjoy it? An exclusively happy heaven that lasts forever simply cannot occur, for you can only know pleasure when you have the perspective of suffering. In other words, there can never be any complete and final satisfaction in this world.

If you ask people whether they're really content, don't just believe their answer. Look and see for yourself: have they really found the end of suffering or are they just putting it off for a while? I see people sick, people dying, people with every imaginable problem. I see happy people too, but I know that the happiness they have is just a pause between occasions of suffering. Eventually, they too will get sick and die. Married couples may be happy for a while, but then they get to the argument stage or the divorce stage, followed by frustration, anger, or depression. Some people have had happy childhoods, but next time around it could be different. Others have had hellish childhoods, and in their next life they may get parents just as bad, or even worse. This sort of reflection should be enough to make you afraid of being reborn. Just because you're smart and make good *kamma* in this life doesn't mean you're going to be free from suffering in the future. Everyone has an enormous store of both good and bad *kamma*; the future is always uncertain.

One of my favorite teachings of the Buddha is the simile of the stick (SN 15:9, 56:33). When I first read it I almost shivered in fear. This simile makes the point that the ripening of *kamma* at death is as uncertain as which end of a stick will hit the ground first when it is thrown into the air. A stick may have a heavy end and a light end, making it more likely to land on the heavy end. But no matter how heavy one end is, there's always a chance the light end will hit the ground first. In the same way, even if you make lots of good *kamma*—by being generous, keeping the precepts, being kind, maintaining a pure mind, and meditating—there's always a possibility that your bad *kamma* will ripen at death. Everybody has a store of bad *kamma*—if not from this life, then from previous lives. Even if your bad *kamma* doesn't ripen when you die this time, as long as you remain in *saṃsāra*, you will eventually experience tremendous suffering—in hell, in the animal realm, and in difficult circumstances as a human. You're only safe if you fully penetrate nonself and become a stream-winner.

Your Sense of Self Is the Root Problem

Saṃsāra is frightening. You can't afford to waste time; you can't mess around. The idea of going back into the world if you've already started to give it up is absolute madness, especially disrobing. The only sensible thing to do is to stay on the path and get your act together. It's not just about getting into *jhāna* or becoming still, although that's a crucial part of it. It's really about seeing and understanding who, or rather what, this person inside actually is. What's always creating agitation, always coming and going? What's frustrated? What's doing the thinking? What's upset? What's angry? What's the source of this? Keep looking in the direction of the experiencer: what feels pain and pleasure? Where does the will come from when "I" choose something? When the mind moves and reaches out for something, what is really reaching out? The more you use the understanding and stillness you've developed in meditation to examine that process, the clearer it becomes.

Be careful not to look out there somewhere, rather than in here—at what you're attached to, rather than where the attachment is emanating from and what's doing the attaching. Look at where things come from, and focus in particular on cause-and-effect relationships. Where do thoughts come from? Keep looking and you'll see that they come from your sense of identity and your desire to bolster and build that identity. It's not, "I think, therefore I am"; it's the other way around: you want to be, therefore you think. You move to create your world, your identity.

When you create something, at first it's very beautiful; but just like in the old fairy tales, all creations turn against their creator in the end. I did a lot to build Bodhinyana Monastery and, if you like, it's my creation. But if I'm not careful, this creation could end up mastering me: I could worry and think about the monastery day and night. If you find a partner and make him yours, at first you think you own him, but after a while you find that he owns you. When you've lost your power and freedom, your creation can turn into a demon that eats away at you. So instead of creating—instead of wanting to be—aspire to stillness. When you become calm and peaceful, the mind becomes even—without bumps, without problems, without suffering, without the need to generate a sense of identity. You calm things down by stilling the creating. When craving—the desire, the will, and the choosing—fades away, agitation also disappears.

If You Want True Happiness, Disappear

Every year I go to the Curtin Medal Awards. I always enjoy those ceremonies—you hear inspiring stories about how people have served and helped our community. A few years ago I was actually given one of those medals. I realized that, as a monk, the more you disappear, the more recognition and awards you get. But because you're disappearing, there really isn't any place to hang the medal. They try to pin the medal on, but it just goes straight through; it doesn't stick, because there's nothing there to stick to.

When you practice this path, you're slowly disappearing. If you understand the idea of vanishing and disappearing—that is, stillness and calm—

you're beginning to understand *anattā*, nonself. This is because the calmer you are, the less you exist—the less there is of a sense of self, a sense of being. This might seem scary, but it's actually beautiful. In fact, it's the only real happiness there is, because the more you let go of the sense of self, the more you're free from suffering in all its forms. And it's that inclination to be free from suffering that drives you deeper on this path. It may take many years or just a few, but in the end the only sensible thing to do is to be patient, stay on this path, and find release in the happiness of disappearing.

In monastic life, part of that disappearing is wearing identical robes and having the same hairstyle. We don't have any insignia to set one monk apart from another. If I didn't stand at the head of the line, no one would know I was the senior monk. We also tend to keep quiet. Why do people talk? They talk to say, "Here I am." By being silent we disappear and fade into the background, until hardly anyone knows we're there, including ourselves. The more you disappear, the happier you are; the more you vanish, the more joy you experience; the less you exist, the more bliss you feel. This tells you what the *Dhamma* is all about. But the words count for nothing compared to the profundity of the experience.

Calming the Will Completely

Eventually you get so still that the mind doesn't move, and you experience the bliss of not being bothered by the will. From those experiences, especially the second *jhāna*, you see clearly that what we call "will" or "choice" is a torturer, like someone who whips you and burns you and rips out your fingernails. But most people cherish the will: they want freedom of choice; they want to follow their desires. They don't realize they are being deceived by their sense of self.

It's wonderful to be sitting in your cave, hut, or room, not wanting anything. If someone asks if there's anything you need, you're not interested. Imagine you have a genie in a bottle who grants you three wishes—any wishes you can think of—and with total honesty, you say, "No thanks." If that happened, you'd have freedom from desire. That freedom is a beautiful state of mind. During a retreat, perhaps you've found yourself sitting in your room or walking on your path, not wanting to be anywhere else in the whole world. What a wonderful feeling that is. That beauty is a result of freedom, of not desiring anything. You don't want to go anywhere; you don't need anything; nothing is missing. When desire vanishes, a state of perfection arises.

You see that desire and the consequent *cetanā*—the will—are part of the manifestation of suffering. The will is the torturer who drives you backward and forward, around and around. Sometimes people try to stop the will, try to stop the thinking. But that very act of trying just encourages the will. Trying to suppress the will only causes more agitation and prevents stillness, peace, and true meditation from happening.

You have to endure doing your duties in the world. But the more you can get away with doing nothing, with having no duties, the better. You may think of this as being lazy, but as long as you're still doing things, you don't really know what "laziness" is. Real "laziness," real rest, isn't your body lying down on a bed, but the *mind* lying down, not doing anything, not creating anything—a mind whose will has been silenced and stopped. When you experience that, you know that real "laziness" is the stillness of the mind, the deep *jhānas* where nothing moves for hours at a time. These are incredible states, where 99 percent of the sense of self has vanished, where there is a rock solid, immovable stillness. Afterward, when you emerge, you realize that the will was silenced, for only when the will is calmed completely can there be an absence of movement. When there's no movement, it's a state of incredible bliss—so profound, so free. You've understood that the will is a torturer that prevents happiness and peace.

The Full Experience of Nonself

There are two citadels of the self delusion: taking yourself to be "the doer" and taking yourself to be "the knower." Most people think knowing and doing is their turf, where they exert complete control. But as you practice this path, you start to see that trying to control even these areas just causes more pain, more difficulty, and more suffering. After a while you realize there's no hope of finding contentment on the path of controlling.

When you begin to appreciate these teachings, you're pulled in a different direction. The will starts to disappear and you feel great; the senses fade and you feel wonderful. Do you get the picture? Has the penny dropped? The experience gradually deepens; you become more still, and more things fade away. You're on the path of the Buddha—the path trodden by the Tathāgata. As more things disappear, you understand that you didn't own them in the first place. You understand that desire is the cause of your suffering, not the way out; that trying to control your world is the cause of suffering, not the solution. You let go of control, the ego fades, the sense of self disappears, things become still, and you vanish. Peace at last. Oh what joy! You've understood nonself.

If you've truly understood nonself, you can call yourself a stream-winner—you're an *ariya*, a noble one on the way out. Once you've seen that there's no one there, you'll never forget it, and that understanding informs every process of your body and mind. You know that the will has nothing to do with you and that the same is true of the five sense-consciousnesses and mind-consciousness. You have no desire to be conscious in order to experience this and that and go here and there.

Why would you want to have more experiences? If you want to see a forest, just look at the trees outside. Trees are trees—that's all. What's the big deal? Someone recently showed me an old picture of some girls who would have turned me on when I was young. They looked yucky now—fashions have changed. A long time ago I saw a picture of my grandfather and grandmother's wedding. My grandmother wore what was supposed to be a really sexy outfit, but it wouldn't turn anyone on these days. It's all just conditioning; it's not real. So don't follow what other people say and do—be rebellious. Look for yourself to see who you are and what happiness truly is.

The Buddha pointed out that what ordinary people say is happiness, the noble ones, the stream-winners, say is suffering; what the noble ones say is happiness, ordinary people say is suffering (Sn.762). The happiness of the noble ones is peace, stillness, and cessation. Take living in a monastery: you get up early, eat one or two meals a day, don't have sex, don't watch television or movies. When someone asks why anyone would do this, the correct answer is that it's happiness. Spending two days, three weeks, or six months by yourself in a hut not talking to other people is called solitary confinement in prison. But what they say is punishment, the *ariyas* say is bliss. If you really had the perspective of a stream-winner, you'd have a completely different way of looking at life: the way of the Buddha.

Once you've seen that you have no core—in any type of consciousness whatsoever or in anything else—then there's nothing you can hold on to as a self. Because you've seen that craving is just an emanation of the sense of self, you no longer find it hard to still the will. And when you still the will, peace arises. The permanent calming of the will—*sabbasaṅkhāra-samatha*—is another way of describing *nibbāna*. The Buddha said there are few beings in the world who can understand the complete calming of the will—you have to be a stream-winner. Be reclusive, sit and do nothing, let go of desire, and be at peace. When you do, you see the path where consciousness fades. Because you delight in the happiness of a fading consciousness, you're often in solitude. When you're in solitude, there's nothing much to be conscious of, nothing much to desire. You're someone with few wishes, not demanding in nature, someone who barely leaves a footprint in the world. Leaving footprints through craving and desire is not your way of walking—you're letting go; you're disappearing.

There comes a time when you disappear entirely. When you have a complete, all-inclusive perception that you're just an empty process, then you give up all attachment to the will and consciousness. There's nothing there; there's nothing to be reborn. You know the seed of rebirth has been destroyed. As it says in the *Ratana Sutta*: "The seed has been destroyed; there is nothing new being created" (Sn. 235). This is experiencing *nibbāna*, the ultimate release and peace.

So turn your mind away from the world—condition it so that you, too, can be free. As Ajahn Chah used to say, there's no point in wandering around the world looking for happiness, searching for the tortoise with the moustache. If you let go, you can be still and peaceful anywhere, any time. Because you're not afraid of stillness, stillness comes. Because you have no fear of disappearing, you're peaceful and free. This is the way to realize nonself, the way to let go of all things, the way to end suffering.

Make This the Last Time 10

♦ ♦ ♦

"I am subject to old age; I am not exempt from old age. I am subject to illness; I am not exempt from illness. I am subject to death; I am not exempt from death. I must be parted and separated from everything dear and agreeable to me..."—this should often be reflected upon by a woman or a man, by a householder or one gone forth. (AN 5:57)

OLD AGE, SICKNESS, AND DEATH are in store for all of us. The younger and healthier you are, the more important this reflection is, since most people find these realities hard to imagine. The truth is, when you get to the age of fifty, you start falling apart, and by sixty you're really going downhill. When you get to seventy, you're sitting in the waiting room, on the way out.

You're Like a Cow Being Led to the Slaughterhouse

My sixtieth year is 2011. Nevertheless, it feels like only yesterday that I was twenty, going out with girls, running around playing soccer, not really worried about my health. A lifetime passes very quickly indeed. It won't be long before I wake up and I'm seventy. This sort of reflection puts our lives in perspective. When we only think of the here and now, we lose sight of the big picture, and we act as if we're intoxicated.

Early in my life, I had a very vivid recurring dream. In the dream I was living with my wife in a hovel, and one morning I woke up and realized what had happened: for years and years I'd been wasting my time, and now I had grown old. With that realization, a powerful feeling of *nibbidā* arose—a sense of repulsion and disgust with what I'd been doing. It's like that story from the *suttas* of the blind man who bought a dirty old rag from a con artist who claimed it was a clean, white cloth. Only when he got his sight back did he realize his mistake (MN 75.23).

One of my favorite stories from the noncanonical Pali scriptures is a story in the *Mahāvaṃsa* about Emperor Asoka's brother. Like most people who enjoy sensual pleasures, the emperor's brother craved power, because power enables you to follow your desires, whatever they may be. He had always hoped that one day he would take over from his brother and become the emperor. But the emperor, who was a devout Buddhist, saw that his brother neither understood nor took an interest in the *Dhamma*, and he decided to teach him a lesson. One day when he was taking a bath, he left all his regalia outside the bathhouse. He had arranged for one of his ministers to walk his brother past the robes and regalia. As they went past the bathhouse, the minister said to Asoka's brother, "Look, the emperor's robes—he must be bathing. You're going to be the emperor one day—why don't you try them on?" Asoka's brother replied, "I can't; it's against the law and would be a capital offense." The minister urged him on: "No, no, it's alright, you can try them on; no one will know." So he did, and because it was a setup, Asoka came straight out of the bathhouse and said, "What are you doing? That's a capital offense! Even though you are my brother, I have to apply the law fairly. I'm sorry, brother, but you will have to be executed."

Asoka then continued, "But since you want to be the emperor so much, and because you are my brother, you can be the emperor for seven days. You can enjoy all the pleasures of the harem, all the food from my kitchens, all the musicians in my court, and anything else you desire. But you can't commute your own sentence, and in seven days I'll execute you." At the end of those seven days, he had his brother brought to him with the executioner waiting. Asoka asked his brother, "Did you enjoy yourself during those seven days?" His brother replied, "How could I enjoy myself when I knew I was going to die in a few days? I couldn't even sleep, let alone enjoy myself." Before setting his brother free, Emperor Asoka drove the lesson home: "Whether it's seven days, seven months, seven years, or twenty-seven years, how can you thoughtlessly immerse yourself in sensual pleasures when you know that death is waiting for you?" This is a powerful lesson for all of us. As it says in the *suttas*, you're like a cow being led to the slaughterhouse (Sn. 580; AN 7:74), inexorably heading in the direction of your own death. Such thoughts should really wake you up.

Reflecting on Old Age, Sickness, and Death

One of the ways to open your eyes to the *Dhamma* is to remember the big picture and see what life is really all about. If you do it properly, it gives rise to that sense of repulsion. I recently read a report about the uprising in Burma in 2007: monks were lined up against a brick wall, and soldiers took hold of their heads and smashed them into the wall, breaking their skulls. Some died, perhaps after hours of agony. Such events may seem far away, but violence can afflict anyone; you could just be in the wrong place at the wrong time. When I was a young monk in Ubon Province in Thailand, the communist armies were just on the other side of the border in Cambodia. One of our monasteries close to the border was shelled. I was about to be sent there by Ajahn Chah, but then he changed his mind; he was afraid a Western monk might be kidnapped or killed by the Khmer Rouge. In any case, the communist troops could have invaded Ubon; anything could've happened. At that moment, death was a live possibility for me; it was an important reminder of the uncertainties of life.

Even if these problems don't exist where you live, keep in mind that the nature of your body is such that sickness could be just around the corner. You might have a cancer inside of you right now that hasn't been detected yet. Are you ready for that sort of news? If you're not ill now, sooner or later you will be—if you last that long. These are realities you should contemplate.

Such reflection allows you to see both the limitations and the opportunities in life—that is, the big picture. When we understand our limitations—old age, sickness, and death—it becomes clear what needs to be done. To see your limitations, look at the nature of the body: it's very fragile, with an endless series of problems that you cannot avoid. So rather than identifying with, indulging in, and caring for this body excessively, you should make sure that this body is your last one and that you don't get into this mess ever again. That's the opportunity.

Unfortunately, delusion tends to rob us of the chance to make use of this opportunity. Most young people are caught by the delusion and intoxication of youth and health. If you're healthy, you think this is the normal state of affairs; if you're young, you think this youth will last forever. Unless you deliberately reflect on the true nature of the body, you easily forget that your actions have consequences, and you end up doing all sorts of stupid things. In life, the pleasures come at the beginning, and if you're not careful you'll pay dearly in the end.

Moreover, everything that is beautiful—whether a flower, a body, or a monastery—will fade and eventually become dirty and disgusting. You can see the cracks in some of the Bodhinyana Monastery buildings already; it's the beginning of the process of the monastery fading, falling apart, and disappearing. All things are like that. Couples may have long marriages, but often they just stay together out of convenience, the pleasure long gone. When you understand that you get the pleasure in the beginning, and that you have to pay for it afterward, you get *nibbidā* toward this entire sensory realm: toward the body, toward relationships, toward coming and going, even toward building monasteries. It's all going to fade away. Even the great earth will eventually be swallowed by the sun, and then there'll be nothing left—no record of human beings, no Great Wall of China, no Taj Mahal, nothing. Everything will be gone—including the teachings of the Buddha. That's just the course of nature.

The suffering and death of close family members is another powerful reminder of the nature of life. The last time I saw my mother, she was suffering from Alzheimer's. She had already been taken away from me—I could see her body, but her mind was gone. As a teenager I saw my father die. I was woken up in the middle of the night by my mother saying she couldn't get him to wake up. I shook him, but it was a dead body. This was my own dad, the one I loved. Even then I knew that this was simply what death was like, and I was able to let go of my father without any sort of wobble in the mind. I was very lucky to come so close to death. You realize that your parents aren't yours anyway; they're just people who looked after you at the beginning of your life. In your past lives, you've had many parents—this is just the latest pair, so why should you be particularly concerned about them? Maybe it's because of this understanding of death that I'm not so attached to the body and my meditation is usually quite good.

My father was only forty-seven when he died, which means I've already lived more than a decade longer than he did. In that sense, I'm on borrowed time. When you think like that, the reality of death becomes very clear, and you get a new and more realistic perspective on life. People who don't reflect like this, which is the vast majority, tend to think that death is far away and that they'll deal with it when it arrives. It's precisely those people who can't accept it when it does.

Old age is a time when most people look back and think about how they've spent their lives. For me, looking back is not at all upsetting, because I've spent over thirty-five years as a monk. That's thirty-five years of leading a pure life, training my mind, and getting the peace and happiness that come from serving others. Of all the people of my age, I have no doubt that I'm among the best prepared for growing old. I look back and think, "Yes, I have used my time wisely." But if, for example, I had led the life of an ordinary married businessman, I wouldn't have the same feeling of peace and security that is gained from having done something really worthwhile. Just as in my recurring dream, one day I might have woken up and thought, "What on earth have I done? I've wasted my time for so long." Reflection on old age, sickness, and death gives us a different perspective on life, which is why we should do it more deeply and more often. When you're doing walking meditation, try using a mantra such as, "I will die, that's for sure; I will die, that's for sure." Even if you're an experienced meditator, don't underestimate the power of the contemplation of death. If you're not a stream-winner, such reflection and meditation has the potential to transform the way you look at the world. Instead of being attracted to the sensory world, you develop *nibbidā* toward it; instead of feeling attachment and craving, you naturally reject it.

Learning How to Die

The final story in my book *Who Ordered This Truckload of Dung?* is about a worm who is so attached to the pile of dung in which he lives that he's unwilling to give it up, even when he's promised a place in heaven. Sometimes I feel that my main activity as a teacher is pulling people out of their own piles of dung. I'm really trying very hard to serve others—writing books, giving talks and interviews—but often people simply prefer to stay in the dung. You pull people out a little bit, and then they decide to crawl back in.

There's great beauty and peace in monastic life, but because they haven't understood suffering, most people don't realize this. Real happiness is found in the freedom of monastic life: having few possessions and no relationships, being unencumbered and not tied down. Most people think of that as suffering. But the *ariyas* say that it's getting involved in the world—having to go to work, worrying about the mortgage—that is true suffering. People worry, "Does she love me? Does she care for me? Is she going to marry me?" and they take that as happiness. I've been there and done that, and I know it's lots and lots of suffering. But people think they need to find out for themselves, so they put their hands in the fire and, of course, get burned. Then they realize that I was right—that the Buddha was right. But it's too late, because now they're entangled in the world.

So be wise and get your life on the right track. Don't just follow what other people do; understand for yourself what the true path to freedom and happiness is, and then follow it. The decision you make is going to affect you, not just today, but in ten, twenty, or thirty years. Ask yourself: are you prepared for old age, sickness, and death? This preparation has nothing to do with your material resources—such as finding a good nursing home—and everything to do with your spiritual resources. Are you able to let go of your health and realize it wasn't your health anyway—that it's just the nature of the body to be sick and weak? You need to learn how to die—how to die to the world, die to your possessions, die to all your hopes of material happiness. That is, you need to learn how to let go of everything. If you learn how to die early on in life, you're on the right track.

In the *Anattalakkhaṇa Sutta*, the Buddha asks the monks whether the five *khandhas*—the body, feeling, perception, will, and consciousness—are permanent or impermanent (SN 22:59). The monks reply that they are impermanent. The Buddha then asks whether something impermanent is happiness or suffering. They reply that it's suffering. He asks if it is appropriate to regard something that is *dukkha* as me, mine, or a self. And the monks say that it's not. When you understand that the *khandhas* are *dukkha*, you realize that one set of *khandhas* is already too much, without having an entire family's worth to worry about. Right there is a great incentive for living the monastic life.

When you understand old age, sickness, and death, you understand that you have a problem, a problem that needs to be solved. The trouble is, most people don't take action until the problem is right in front of them. Only when they get old will they try to do something about old age; only when they actually get sick will they be concerned about sickness; only when they're about to die will they think about dying. They're just like those kids who should've been studying for months and instead do all their reading the night before the exam. It's the same with the great exams of old age, sickness, and death: do your homework now, while you're still young, healthy, and fully alive.

Reflecting on Sensual Desires

You can prepare for those exams by abandoning concern for bodies—your own and those of others. When you look at a really attractive person, you just see another being in *saṃsāra* who is subject to the same old age, sickness, and death as you. When I see a woman, I see her no differently from the way I see a fellow monk. She's just a being in a woman's body, not an object of desire. It's wonderful when you can look at all people like that. It means you're free.

Some of our desires make us so fevered that we can't stop thinking, fantasizing, and wasting so much time. Still, people enjoy that feeling. It's like the simile of the leper who burns his itchy wounds over a fire because it makes him feel a little bit better (MN 75.17). He's actually burning himself, but because of the nature of his affliction, he perceives it as pleasurable. It's the same with sensual pleasures. If we understood their true nature, we would let go of them.

Ajahn Sumedho once told a story about a couple who lived near Chithurst Monastery in England. They had a supposedly perfect marriage: they fell in love when they were young and hardly ever argued. Then the wife got terrible arthritis and ended up in constant pain. But when she wanted to let go and die, her husband wouldn't let her, saying he couldn't stand living without her. So one partner had to suffer because the other one wouldn't let her go. The previous happiness of that relationship was like a debt that now had to be repaid.

Indeed, the Buddha said that having sensory desire is like taking out a loan (MN 39.14): whatever pleasure you withdraw from the sensory world, you have to pay back with disappointment, frustration, and suffering. You can see it when people fall in love: if they get rejected by their beloveds, they're broken-hearted, devastated, or even suicidal. You might get some happiness when you first fall in love, but you'll pay for it later.

As you keep reflecting, "I must be parted and separated from everything dear and agreeable to me," you gradually lose interest in sensory pleasures and the body. When you thoroughly investigate them, you realize that it just doesn't make sense to pursue happiness in these things. You can then commit yourself to being free from the body and making sure you don't get any other bodies in the future. You understand that attachment to the body is one of the most crucial things to understand and let go of.

Reflecting on the Body

To overcome attachment to the body, we do practices such as the contemplation of the thirty-one parts of the body. In Thailand, you might even go to see an autopsy. Of all the autopsies I've seen—and I've seen some gross ones—the one that shook me the most was that of a young man of the same age as me. Because he was my age, I could identify with his body. As the autopsy unfolded I saw the repulsive nature of that body, and I knew that mine had to be the same. It drove the message home: there is no value in attaching to the body.

When you see this sort of thing, you recognize that the body's nature is to get old, get sick, and die. When that understanding penetrates deeply, you have gained insight into some of the greatest suffering of human existence. Indeed, it was reflecting on old age, sickness, and death that made the Buddha become a monk and set out in search of freedom from these things (MN 26.13). He realized that old age, sickness, and death are basically forms of torture, and it gave him the motivation to find a way out.

When you contemplate your body in this way, it gives you a feeling of repulsion toward it, and the attachment to it—the concern, the involvement, the infatuation—disappears. When the infatuation with your own body disappears, the infatuation with others' bodies also disappears. You look at a pretty girl, and all you see is a body with the same heart, lungs, and limbs that you have. You get a natural restraint of the senses, and lust does not arise.

This sort of reflection can also be used to counter ill will. You're less likely to get angry and upset with someone who has cancer; you have a natural sympathy for someone who is in pain and suffering and about to die. You can extend those feelings to anyone, since we're all dying. No matter what people say or do to you, just remind yourself that they're dying. When you look at other people like this, the hindrance of ill will just doesn't arise. Because lust and ill will do not arise and you're not concerned with the body, you can peacefully sit down, close your eyes, and enter the realm of the mind.

Freedom from the Body

So the reason you do body contemplation is to understand the body's true nature, to get *nibbidā* toward it, and to enable you to abandon it. You think, "Good riddance," when the hands disappear; "About time," when your legs go; "What a relief," when the whole back disappears; "Whoopee," when the breath fades away. The whole body just vanishes. At last you're free from it. And because you've let go of your body, you've had a preview of the proper way to die. This is one of the great teachings we get from deep meditation.

If you can't let go of the body when you're healthy, how do you suppose you're going to do it when you're sick and in pain? Even now, when you've got aches and pains in the body, is it easy to meditate? Is it easy to watch the breath? What do you reckon it's going to be like when you're sick, in pain, and dying, when you're weak and haven't got much energy left? It's much, much harder then. So while you have the health, while the body is reasonably okay—or whatever state it's in, because it's only going to get worse—now is the time to learn to let it go.

Train yourself: sit down, cross your legs, close your eyes, and practice present-moment awareness and silence. Remember that most of your thinking is about the body and the world of sensory pleasure. Stop all of that. Stay with your breathing, and allow the breath to become beautiful and the body to disappear. As you're focusing fully on the breath, you can't feel your head or your legs. You don't know where the body is and you couldn't care less; it has disappeared and all you have is the breath. The breath becomes beautiful, and then a *nimitta* arises. At that point the body, including the breath, has completely vanished.

Freedom from the body: this is what happens when you die. The *nimitta* is the same light that people see when they leave their bodies at death or have a near-death experience. The *nimitta* stage is wonderfully blissful—better than sex, better than a relationship—and it's not that hard to achieve when you let go of the body. It's only when you're still attached to the body that it's hard. If you see that attachment is still there, remind yourself that you're actually attached to suffering, that you're just holding on to hot coals. Let the body go, drop it, and get out of the pile of dung.

If you haven't experienced these things, it can all sound like a fantasy. But as your meditation improves, you gradually start to realize that this is not a fantasy, that these states do exist, and that what I'm saying is valid. All you need to do is take your meditation further and drop more of the body. As you practice in this way, you start to bliss out. You understand that the body isn't just suffering because of old age, sickness, and death, but even its normal state is a huge heap of suffering. This is one of the incredibly powerful realizations you get from deep meditation. A *nimitta* is enough to give you this realization, but if you get into *jhāna* it's unmistakably clear.

Because we've become so used to hurting all the time, we normally don't recognize the suffering of the body. Ajahn Chah gave a wonderful simile of a person being born with a rope tied around the neck and two demons pulling on the rope from either side. He never actually said what the demons were, but I think of them as desire and ill will, or as the will and attachment to the body. The demons continuously pull that rope tight, but because it's always been tight and you've never been able to breathe properly, you don't realize what's going on. You think this is normal, that this is life. Then one day you have a decent meditation, you get to the beautiful breath stage, and the rope loosens. You can breathe and you think, "Wow, it's so peaceful, it's so nice." Then you get to the *nimitta* stage and the rope loosens almost completely: "Wow, this is really amazing!"

You're realizing a great truth of Buddhism, something the Buddha also realized: the reason you're happy is because a whole heap of suffering is gone. The demons have let go of the rope, and you can breathe again. It's wonderful when you experience this for yourself, because it gives you direct insight into what we're trying to achieve. Because of the painful nature of the body, we practice to detach from and transcend it, by going into the realm of the mind. When you do this fully and irreversibly, you become a nonreturner, and you'll never again be reborn in the world of physical bodies. But if you don't get your meditation together, who knows where your next rebirth will be.

The Door to the Deathless Is Open

You too can experience the bliss of freedom. Then you'll understand the Buddha's teachings and become independent. You won't need other people, and you won't care what they say or do. You'll just sit down in solitude, bliss out, and become free. Don't you want that? It's on offer, and you can do it. If you haven't done it yet, it's just a matter of time. The door to the deathless is open. It's up to you to walk through that door, and then you won't grow old, get sick, or die ever again. Make this the last time.

Climbing the Pyramid of Samādhi

11

◆ ◆ ◆

A JAHN TATE was one of the monks I loved the most, one who really looked like an *arahant*. I will never forget the vision of him in his monastery in Nong Kai Province on the banks of the Mekong River. The king of Thailand had built a big hall for him—in Thai they call it a *mandapa*—and it was very, very extravagant for a forest monastery. I will always remember going into that hall. It was beautifully designed with a lovely view over the river, and there in a corner, sitting in a chair, was this old monk. The way he looked and the aura around him suggested that this was a very peaceful person, a holy monk. He seemed to really belong at the foot of a tree with just leaves and branches over him. But he'd been put in this place by the king—it was his fate, if you like.

Before I went to see him, I'd been thinking of all the questions I would ask this great monk. But when I approached him, they all dropped away, which in a sense made my journey there look pointless. Instead of asking a question, I said something that was actually quite wise: that it's much better if we don't ask questions but find out the answers for ourselves. That made him smile; he said, "Yes, that's the right attitude." Instead of relying on other people, we should find out the truth for ourselves and take responsibility for our own virtue, our own peace, and our own wisdom.

Keep It Simple

These days we're often exposed to information overload. Many of us have a huge number of talks compressed into MP3s on our iPods. At our monastery we've got all the *suttas* in Pali, Chinese, Thai, and English, and even some in German. They're also available on the computer in our office. There's so much *Dhamma* available that sometimes you wonder how much is actually needed. At the time of the Buddha, people would have heard perhaps only a single *sutta*, and for some that was enough to see the truth and gain happiness and balance in their lives. But these days many people devour information. Just as many people's bodies are overweight and obese because they eat too much, so too, many people's brains are overweight and obese because they ingest too much information. Unless we know how to deal with all that information, it may only confuse us. We need to remember that the essence of the teachings of the Buddha is clear and simple: don't do anything bad, do what is good, and purify the mind (Dhp. 183). This in turn boils down to just one thing: the path of kindness, peace, and harmony. The simple teachings are often the very best.

As Buddhists, then, we're committed to kindness and following the precepts. And we can't just think about these things; we actually have to practice them. Only then do they lead to peace, freedom, and harmony. It's what we *do* that matters, and we know the right things to do by their results. That's why the Buddha told the venerable Upāli that one knows that something is in accordance with the *Dhamma*, in accordance with the right path, if it leads to a beautiful sense of freedom and peace (AN 7:83).

The sense of freedom and peace that builds up as you practice correctly is a mental experience, since physical suffering is unavoidable. When things happen in the world, the mind just looks on and knows that this is the nature of *saṃsāra* and that *saṃsāra* is suffering. You see the suffering without reacting to it, just standing there in the midst of it, as it were.

In the *suttas*, the great *arahants* say that the world is simply suffering arising and suffering passing away (SN 12:15). These great *arahants* were often unrecognizable: they would go on almsround, eat their food, do their chores, go to bed at night, and wake up in the morning. Because they fit into the community and didn't stand out, they almost disappeared into the background. That sort of evenness, that levelness, is part of the middle way of practice. Whatever leads to a state of happiness, stillness, and peace is the proper path.

The Happiness of Virtue and Restraint

You can teach people to practice virtue and keep the precepts, but in the end you don't know what people actually do. All you can do is show them what the Buddha did, what the Kruba Ajahns do, and what the *suttas* say: if you want to have a happy and peaceful life, you must restrain the defilements. Whether you're a monk or a layperson, if you indulge in sensual pleasures, you will wear down your spiritual power and get dragged down into the ways of the world. People who indulge in such pleasures may appear happy on the outside, but if you look deeper you see something else. There's a great saying of George Bernard Shaw, who when asked why it is that believers seem happier than nonbelievers, replied that it's no different from a drunken person appearing happier than a sober one. It's the same for the world of the five senses. Pursuing pleasure by watching movies, going to parties, having sex, or whatever, is like being drunk on the five senses. It's a form of delusion, and you have to pay for it later. You're borrowing happiness, and afterward you experience negativity, anxiety, or even depression.

In such *suttas* as the *Sāmaññaphala Sutta* (DN 2.63), the Buddha said that anyone who keeps good moral conduct experiences *anavajjasukha*, the happiness of blamelessness. It's wonderful to experience the truth of such teachings in your own practice. When you keep the precepts, restrain yourself, and do the right thing for a long period of time, you feel really good about yourself. You haven't done things that others don't know about, thinking you're clever because you've indulged in secret pleasures. Such things are never really secret anyway, because *you* know and *you* care. You don't necessarily feel guilty or punish yourself, but you miss out on the happiness that comes from the freedom born of blamelessness. If you look carefully at your life, you'll be able to observe the effects of your actions on your level of happiness, peace, and freedom.

Restraint also gives you a feeling of power. That's been my experience every time I've given something up and restrained my desires, whether as a monk or a layperson. That's how I felt when I gave up alcohol as a student. You feel the power of not yielding to the defilements—you've kicked their butt and you're free from them. It's literally like being released from prison or bondage. The more you indulge in the five senses, the more you tie yourself up in shackles. But the more you stop the greed, hatred, and delusion, the more you are following the path of the *ariyas* and the more happiness and peace you experience.

Ask yourself how the Buddha would've practiced, what Mahāmoggallāna or Sāriputta would've done. If you follow the example of the great monks and nuns in the *suttas*, you can't go wrong. You'll get an even and happy mind, because you're resisting, letting go, and overcoming the causes of suffering in life.

So when you start to practice virtue, your level of happiness increases. Because you have greater happiness, your mindfulness increases, you feel more peaceful, and your meditation improves. It all comes together when you start to experience happiness. Happiness also gives you a sense of contentment. Contentment is the result of restraint, because your mind is less enslaved by desire. Please recognize the happiness of the freedom *from* desire, as opposed to the slavery *of* desire. In the world, you're constantly pulled along by the nose: a beautiful woman or a handsome man comes along and you just have to look. Sooner or later you're going out together and then you're caught. You're put in handcuffs: the engagement ring and the wedding ring. Then you're stuck for years. Marriages often break up, and then you may have to pay alimony, perhaps for the rest of your life. So be careful what you do if you want to retain any real freedom.

Be the Master of Your Desires

Initially, when you're caught up in the world, you think you own your desires and have control over them. But if you indulge, you'll find that the desires soon control you. Instead of having a choice, you're now compelled to satisfy them. A long time ago I saw the play *Waiting for Godot*.

In this play, one of the characters has a dog. In the first part of the play, he leads the dog around. In the second part of the play, the dog is the master and the "owner" has to walk on all fours with a collar and leash. One of the themes of the play is that master and slave usually swap places, and the same is true of our relationship with craving. We start off thinking we're in control of our cravings and desires, that we can bend them to our will and purpose, but before we realize it, cravings and desires and the moods of the mind control us instead.

To gain freedom we must use restraint; we have to say no to desires and cravings. When we say no to indulging in sensory experiences, we feel a marvelous sense of freedom: we're no longer enslaved by those experiences. If you can't get any sleep because you're taking an overnight flight, it's great to know that you don't have to have that sleep; you can deal with it. It's nice to get your daily meal, but if you don't, it doesn't bother you all that much. So even though the Buddha didn't really recommend fasting, sometimes it's good to fast for a day, just to find out if you're still in charge of your desires.

Many years ago I decided to give up tea for the whole three-month rains retreat. As soon as I had announced it, one of the monks I was living with at the time came to see me with great concern, because he knew this was a great sacrifice for an Englishman. A few years before, another English monk had done the same thing and he had found it very difficult. I replied that I was determined to have a nice time without tea, and in the end it really didn't affect me much. So sometimes it's nice to loosen the grip of your desires. The less you have and the less you need, the freer you are. You know that these things don't own you; it's you who owns them.

If you have restraint, if you can say no to cravings and desires, not only do you gain an incredible sense of freedom and peace but also a wonderful sense of confidence. This is actually mentioned in the *suttas*: if you're virtuous, if you keep the precepts, you can go anywhere without fear (DN 16.1.24). And because your desires are not in charge of you, you're flexible and able to adapt to changing circumstances. So sense restraint gives rise to confidence and a marvelous feeling of independence.

You should aim to acquire the freedom, peace, and happiness born of virtue and a good heart. But don't allow virtue to become an imposition on you. When you understand virtue properly, you know it's about freedom from suffering. Like an infant who puts his hand in a fire, we experience pain when we do the wrong thing. But just as that infant learns from his experience and doesn't put his hand in a fire again, so we should be observant enough to see the effects of our actions. If we're not, we'll remain in the power of craving, ill will, guilt, and other defilements, and just create more pain and hurt for ourselves. True virtue, on the other hand, creates peace, freedom, and happiness. It's the same with meditation: if you're truly letting go and pacifying the mind, that too leads to these beautiful qualities.

The Pyramid of Samādhi and Insight

The Buddha said—and this is part of the chanting at a monastic ordination—that when *samādhi* is empowered by virtue, it has great benefit and great fruit (DN 16.1.12). The Buddha is actually saying that without restraining the defilements and committing to doing the right thing, *samādhi* is weak. When people think about meditation, they often wonder how they should watch the breath, what they should do when a *nimitta* arises, and how other technical aspects of the meditation process work; but they rarely ask what fuels *samādhi*. It can be easy to forget that virtue and restraint are immensely important for success in *samādhi*.

The *Tāyana Sutta* (SN 2:8) says that you cannot reach oneness of mind, *samādhi*, without abandoning the five senses and sensual desire. That's an important teaching. We know that the world of the five senses is suffering by its very nature and inevitably leads to problems and difficulties. When I work to maintain the monastery or lead the *Sangha*, I know it's going to be full of suffering, because it all falls within the world of sights, sounds, smells, tastes, and touches. It's always a struggle to keep these things afloat; I don't expect it to be easy just because I'm in charge. The reality is that you cannot escape suffering in the five-sense world, and thus there's only one solution: you have to let it go. The sole purpose of meditation—the process leading up to *samādhi*—is to calm the five senses and make the mind peaceful. It's only from peace and stillness, from letting go, that you get a realistic perspective on the world.

As a young man, I traveled to Central America. I traveled through the jungle of the Yucatan Peninsula, and then I climbed one of the ancient Mayan pyramids. For the first time in days, I could see beyond my immediate surroundings and get a wider view of where I was. This is an excellent simile for what happens in meditation. When you get into a proper state of *samādhi*, your mind becomes so clear that, for the very first time, you can look down with a clear perspective upon the world in which you've been struggling.

This is an important aspect of wisdom. When you step outside of your ordinary self, you can accurately view and assess what you've been doing all this time. You can see that although you thought you were being wise, often you were not. Although you thought you were doing good in the world, at times you were actually harming yourself and others. When I was trekking through the jungle, I couldn't see where I was going and it was a hard slog. But high up on that pyramid, I could see where the best paths were, the shortest and easiest routes. In the same way, when you have a proper meditation experience, you understand what the world is, and you realize the most peaceful, problem-free path to get through the jungle of life.

When you see clearly, you stop expecting things from life that it will never be able to give. That's my definition of suffering: expecting from life what it can never provide. If you want too much from life, you suffer. You create that suffering with your expectation. When you understand the limitations of life and the limitations of your abilities, you know that all you can do is try your best to be helpful and not harm others. But even with the best of intentions, sometimes you won't succeed. That's life; you can't do anything about it. A wise sensitivity to the world around you comes from seeing things as they truly are—seeing that the nature of the jungle is harm and suffering. Right now, we all have old age, sickness, and death latent in our bodies. This is the nature of bodies. All we can do is accept it and be at peace with it.

The Buddha said we are all pierced by two arrows of suffering: the physical arrow and the mental arrow (SN 36:6). The physical arrow is the suffering connected with the body, which you can't do much about. What you can do is remove the mental arrow. The mental arrow is the attitude of "I don't want this," "It shouldn't be this way," "Why is it this way?" When you stand on top of that pyramid and look over your life and over the world, you get a clear and realistic perspective. When you come down from the pyramid, you're far wiser. Because you're wise, your life is peaceful and easy, and the only suffering you experience is from the physical arrow. It's the nature of wisdom that it gives you the best possible life.

People have all sorts of ideas about the *nimitta*, *jhāna*, the nature of existence, the four noble truths, and dependent origination. Even though they usually don't know what they're talking about, they still keep on speculating. But the Buddha said that he only taught suffering and the end of suffering (SN 22:86), and that's really all we need to focus on. By doing so, we're focusing on the way to peace and happiness. And that way is learning how to leave the world by climbing the pyramid inside the heart: the pyramid of meditation. Climbing that pyramid enables you to know the characteristics of wisdom: the knowledge of the middle way of balance, gentleness, happiness, and peace. When you see that big picture, you become free. And the sign of freedom is a beautiful, peaceful life. Sure, you still have physical problems, but a whole heap of suffering—the mental arrow—has been removed.

The Beautiful Middle Way

We've all had enough physical and mental suffering. Although we sometimes try to lessen the physical suffering in one way or another, we realize that such suffering is just part of having a body, part of living in the world. It's also part of life to see people do stupid things, hurting themselves and others. Living in Australia, I often see kangaroos fighting over the monastery's leftover food. You notice how greedy they are, just like human beings. But since you know that's the nature of the world and that you can't do anything about it, you just smile and let it go. In the same way, although you can only do so much about other people's suffering, you can pull out your own mental arrow and learn how to be at peace. Then you know that the only way suffering is fully eliminated is through the freedom of never being reborn again. In the end, that's the only thing you can wish for. And indeed, wishing *nibbāna* for yourself and others is the highest form of loving kindness.

The *Ratana Sutta* says the Buddha attained *nibbāna* for the maximum benefit of other beings (Sn. 233). In other words, the best possible gift you can give to others is for you yourself to become enlightened. If you aspire to true altruism, that's what you should be focusing on. Unless you're enlightened, you don't really know what you're doing. It's only when you climb that pyramid in the heart called meditation and get all the way to the top that you learn how the problems of life are overcome. It's when you go beyond the world and see the big picture—the bird's-eye view, the *ariyan* view—that you understand how it all works. When you understand, when you become a stream-winner, you marvel at how you could have missed it for all those years. You've gained the wisdom that sees very clearly what creates peace and happiness—a wisdom that doesn't aim for perfection, that never asks for what the world can't give. Because of its clarity, that wisdom is able to lessen suffering. Please remember that suffering is asking the world for something it just can't give you.

So climb that pyramid and look from above. This simple metaphor can help you understand the feeling of true meditation, the taste of wisdom and enlightenment, and how you can achieve them. When you understand this, you see the meaning of the Buddhist path, the meaning of the simple teachings of virtue, stillness, and wisdom. Once you've achieved that great wisdom, you can be at peace no matter what happens to your body. You still look after it, but you don't go over the top because you know its nature. You practice the beautiful middle way.

A person who practices the middle way is a person who gradually disappears. Only when you stay in the middle is it possible to vanish. If you're too extreme in any way—too tall or too short, too fat or too thin—you stand out. That is what's so brilliant about the image of Ajahn Tate in Thailand. He was in a magnificent palace, but he had vanished. When I went into that room, it seemed empty—I had to look twice to see the little old monk sitting in the corner. So your job is to do just that: be like Ajahn Tate and disappear from this world of suffering.

Abbreviations

✦ ✦ ✦ ————————————————————

AN	*Aṅguttara Nikāya*
Dhp.	*Dhammapada*
DN	*Dīgha Nikāya*
MN	*Majjhima Nikāya*
SN	*Saṃyutta Nikāya*
Sn.	*Sutta Nipāta*
Thī.	*Therīgāthā*
Ud.	*Udāna*

For the *Dīgha Nikāya, Majjhima Nikāya, Saṃyutta Nikāya,* and *Aṅguttara Nikāya* (forthcoming), references are to the sutta numbering scheme used in the English translation published by Wisdom Publications. Otherwise the numbering scheme used is that of the Pali texts published by the Pali Text Society.

Glossary

✦ ✦ ✦ ――――――――――――――――――――――――――――――――――

Ajahn Chah (1918–92). A Thai monk regarded by many as one of the greatest Thai meditation masters of the twentieth century.

Ajahn Jagaro. An early Western disciple of Ajahn Chah and the first abbot of Bodhinyana Buddhist Monastery, from 1983 to 1995.

Ajahn Sumedho. The first Western disciple of Ajahn Chah.

Ajahn Tate. A disciple of Ajahn Mun, who is widely seen as the father of the modern movement known as the Thai Forest Tradition. Ajahn Tate is himself widely regarded as one of the most accomplished Thai meditation masters in the modern era.

anāgāmī. Nonreturner, one who has attained the third stage of enlightenment.

anagārika. Literally, "a homeless one." In Western Theravada monasteries this is taken to mean someone who keeps the eight precepts and is in training to ordain as a novice monk.

anālaya. Detachment, nonreliance; literally, "non-roosting." It is the fourth term in the third noble truth describing the cessation of craving.

ānāpānasati. Mindfulness of breathing. The *Ānāpānasati Sutta*, MN 118, is the Buddha's main instruction on meditation on the breath.

anattā. Nonself, the absence of a permanent self.

anavajjasukha. The happiness of blamelessness. The happiness that comes from living a virtuous life.

arahant. A fully enlightened one; the fourth stage of enlightenment.

ariya. A noble one, a person who has attained at least the level of a stream-winner, the first of the four stages of enlightenment.

āruppa. Immaterial, as in the immaterial attainments.

āsava. Literally, "outflowings"; that is, the mind "flowing out" into the world. The *suttas* usually enumerate three types of *āsavas*: (1) *kāmāsava*, outflowing due to sensual desire; (2) *bhavāsava*, outflowing due to (craving for) existence; (3) *avijjāsava*, outflowing due to ignorance or delusion.

attā. Self or ego.

Bodhinyana Buddhist Monastery. The monastery in Perth, Australia, at which Ajahn Brahm is the abbot.

cetanā. Intention or will.

dependent origination. This teaching shows, through a chain of twelve links, how suffering is rooted in delusion.

Dhamma. The teachings of the Buddha; the truth; how things actually are.

dukkha. Suffering.

eightfold path, the noble. (1) right view or understanding; (2) right thoughts or intentions; (3) right speech; (4) right action; (5) right livelihood; (6) right effort; (7) right mindfulness; (8) right stillness, i.e., *jhāna*.

four noble truths. The four noble truths are the main teaching framework of Buddhism. They are: (1) suffering; (2) the cause of suffering; (3) the cessation of suffering; (4) the path leading to the cessation of suffering.

hindrances, the five. (1) sensual desire; (2) ill-will and anger; (3) lethargy and dullness; (4) restless and remorse; (5) doubt.

indriya. Faculty or power. The standard set of five faculties is: (1) *saddhā*, faith; (2) *viriya*, energy; (3) *sati*, mindfulness; (4) *samādhi*, stillness; (5) *paññā*, wisdom.

jhāna. The deep meditation states of stillness and letting go.

kamma. Action or activity created by volition. Sometimes *kamma* is used more loosely to include the results of actions.

kāmacchanda. Desire for the world of the five senses.

khandha. Aggregate. The *suttas* list five groups of mental and physical phenomena that are to be investigated in terms of the three characteristics. They are as follows: (1) *rūpa*, body; (2) *vedanā*, feeling; (3) *saññā*, perception; (4) *saṅkhāras*, willed activities (of body, speech, and mind); (5) *viññāṇa*, consciousness.

Kruba Ajahn. A senior teacher in the Thai Forest Tradition.

Mahāvaṃsa. A post-canonical Pali work that chronicles the early history of Sri Lanka. It has been translated by Wilhelm Geiger as *The Mahāvaṃsa or the Great Chronicle of Ceylon* (London: Pali Text Society, 1912). The story of Asoka and his brother told at the beginning of chapter 10 has been adapted from Geiger's translation.

Māra. Literally, "the killer." Often called "the Evil One," Māra is a tempter figure who seeks to keep beings bound to the round of rebirth. Māra is also used in the *suttas* in a metaphorical sense as the personification of defilements.

mettā. Loving kindness, the wish that someone may experience happiness and peace.

nāmarūpa. An umbrella term for all the mental and physical aspects of a being except consciousness.

nibbāna. Literally "extinguishment," as in the going out of a flame. It is the supreme goal for Buddhists, the destruction of greed, hatred, and delusion, and the end of all suffering.

nibbidā. Aversion, repulsion, revulsion, or weariness, especially toward the round of existence. This is a natural consequence of deep insight and has nothing to do with unwholesome states.

nimitta. In the context of Buddhist meditation, a mental image, particularly a brilliant light seen in the mind's eye.

nirāmisa sukha. Lit. "noncarnal happiness." This is another term for the happiness of deep *samādhi*, in particular of *jhāna*.

nirodha. Cessation.

Nong Kai Province. A province in northeast Thailand.

paññā. Wisdom.

pabhassara citta. Radiant mind; see, e.g., AN 1:49–52.

Pali. Language related to Sanskrit in which the Buddha's teachings were recorded, at first orally and later in writing.

paṭinissagga. Letting go, abandoning, forfeiting.

parinibbāna. Complete extinguishment; usually refers to the termination of the lifespan of the Buddha or an *arahant.*

sabbasaṅkhārasamatha. The full stilling of the *kamma*-producing will.

saddhā. Faith or confidence.

samādhi. Sustained attention on one thing; stillness.

samatha. Calming. Often refers to meditation techniques whose end result is *jhāna,* the deep meditation states of letting go.

sammāsaṅkappa. Right thought or intention, the second factor in the noble eightfold path.

saṃsāra. Literally, "wandering on"—the continuous round of death and rebirth.

Sangha. The community of ordained disciples of the Lord Buddha; the third of the three refuges for all Buddhists.

saṅkhāra. In general *sutta* usage it means the will; see SN 22:57. Sometimes it is used to refer to that which is conditioned or has arisen dependent on causes.

sati-sampajañña. Mindfulness and clear comprehension.

sīla. Virtue or moral conduct.

sotāpanna. Stream-winner, the first stage of enlightenment. A person who is guaranteed to attain full enlightenment within seven lifetimes at the most.

stream-winner. See *sotāpanna.*

sutta. A discourse of the Buddha or one of his main monastic disciples.

Tathāgata. A term the Buddha uses to refer to himself.

Tipiṭaka. The three-part canon of Buddhist scriptures.

Ubon Province. The province in northeast Thailand where Wat Pah Pong is located.

upādāna. Taking up, holding on, or attaching.

upasama. Stillness, peace.

vinaya. The section of the Buddhist canon containing the rules of conduct for monks and nuns and the procedures for the proper functioning of the *Sangha*.

virāga. Fading away, detachment, absence of lust, dispassion. *Virāga* is a consequence of deep insight—the "seeing of things as they really are"—and the consequent experience of repulsion from *saṃsāra*.

Wat Pah Nanachat. The International Forest Monastery in northeast Thailand. An offshoot of Ajahn Chah's monastery Wat Pah Pong, this monastery was established in 1975 by a small group of Western monks that included Ajahn Sumedho and Ajahn Brahm. It was set up specifically to train non-Thai monks, and it remains the only monastery in Thailand of this kind to the present day.

Wat Pah Pong. The monastery in northeast Thailand established by Ajahn Chah. This monastery is now the central monastery of the over 300 monasteries that are connected to Ajahn Chah.

Index

About the Author

♦ ♦ ♦

AJAHN BRAHM was born in London in 1951. At age sixteen, he began regarding himself as a Buddhist after reading books on the subject, and his interest in Buddhism and meditation flourished while studying theoretical physics at Cambridge University. He was ordained as a monk at age twenty-three and subsequently spent nine years studying and training in the forest meditation tradition under the renowned meditation master Ven. Ajahn Chah.

In 1983 he was invited to help establish a forest monastery near Perth in Western Australia, and he is now the abbot of Bodhinyana Monastery and the spiritual director of the Buddhist Society of Western Australia. In 2004 Ajahn Brahm was awarded the prestigious John Curtin Medal for vision, leadership, and community service. A highly sought-after speaker around the world, he attracts thousands to his inventive and insightful talks.

About Wisdom

✦ ✦ ✦ ————————————————————————————

WISDOM PUBLICATIONS is dedicated to offering works relating to and inspired by Buddhist traditions. To learn more about us or to explore our other books, please visit our website at www.wisdompubs.org. You can subscribe to our e-newsletter or request our print catalog online, or by writing to:

Wisdom Publications
199 Elm Street
Somerville, Massachusetts 02144 USA
617-776-7416, or info@wisdompubs.org.

Wisdom is a nonprofit, charitable 501(c)(3) organization, and donations in support of our mission are tax deductible.

Wisdom Publications is affiliated with the Foundation for the Preservation of the Mahayana Tradition (FPMT).